AUDITION ARSENAL FOR WOMEN IN THEIR 20s

101 Monologues by Type,
2 Minutes & Under

A Smith and Kraus Book
Published by Smith and Kraus, Inc.
177 Lyme Road, Hanover, NH 03755
www.smithandkraus.com

First Edition: August 2005
10 9 8 7 6 5 4 3 2 1

Manufactured in the United States of America
Text Design by Julia Gignoux, Freedom Hill Design
Cover Design by Alex Karan of Blaise Graphics, www.blaisegraphics.com

The Library of Congress Cataloging-In-Publication Data
Audition arsenal for women in their 20s ; 101 monologues by type, 2 minutes and under / edited by Janet B. Milstein. —1st ed.
p. cm. — (Monologue audition series)
Includes bibliographical references.
ISBN-10 1-57525-396-8 ISBN-13: 978-1-57525-396-1
1. Monologues. 2. Acting—Auditions. I. Milstein, Janet B. II. Series.

PN2080.A77 2005
813'.045089287—dc22
2005044119

AUDITION ARSENAL
FOR WOMEN IN THEIR 20s

101 Monologues by Type, 2 Minutes & Under

EDITED BY JANET B. MILSTEIN

MONOLOGUE AUDITION SERIES

A Smith and Kraus Book

Acknowledgments

I would like to express my deepest gratitude to
Eric Kraus and Marisa Smith for entrusting me with this project
and for their wisdom, patience, and generosity.

I would also like to thank the following people
for their help and support:

Karen Milstein
Barbara Lhota
The Milsteins
Alex Karan
Russ Tutterow
Sandy Shinner
Keith Huff
Karen Vesper
Tom Volo
Julia Gignoux
Susan Moore

All of the wonderful actors who took the time to give their input
and all of the talented writers who shared their work with me.

Contents

ANGRY/FED UP

PERSUASIVE/INSPIRATIONAL

HIGH-STRUNG/NEUROTIC/STRESSED-OUT

LOST/CONFUSED/TRYING TO MAKE SENSE

SEXUAL/FLIRTATIOUS

Audition Arsenal Introduction

Redefining the monologue book

When Eric Kraus approached me about editing a new series of monologue books based on character type, some questions immediately came to mind: Was this type as in theater or film? Most specific types fall under film, yet monologues are rarely used for film or on-camera. For theater there are really only three main types: Leading Man/Lady, Ingénue/Young Man, and Character Actors. If I wanted to offer more detailed types, what criteria would be most useful? Would profession be considered a type? How about funny? Could social status define type?

In addition, I considered what was needed in a monologue book that had not yet been addressed. How would I improve upon the monologue books I own? What would make a book more valuable? How could I create a book to solve the problems my students are constantly voicing? As an actor, writer, and monologue coach, I wanted this new monologue series to give actors what they truly need for auditions. I had my own ideas about what *I* would find useful, but I decided to poll some actors to get their input, as well. The actors had a lot of common requests that confirmed my initial instincts. Most importantly this series would need to maximize the number of monologues an actor would actually use from one source. To do that, the traditional monologue book would need to be reinvented.

How are the books in this series better?

When I was studying acting in college, I'd always wished that there were monologue books just for actors in their twenties. And my dream books would have taken it a step further and been separated by gender to increase the number of monologues in one book that specifically applied to me. Now, I am presenting that to you — Women 20s, Men 20s, Women 30s, and Men 30s. No more skipping over pages and pages because the characters are out of your age range or not for your gender. Within each book, the choices are plentiful, and you're sure to find pieces that fit your specific needs.

That brings me to the next revolutionary feature of the Audition Arsenal series: The books are organized by type. By type, I'm referring to the most prominent quality the monologue reveals about the actor. So instead of being typed somewhat generically (e.g., waitress or Ingénue), the monologues are designed to show you possess the qualities crucial to a particular character or role. Auditioning for a Harry Kondoleon play? Check out the High-strung/Neurotic/Stressed-Out category. Want to get a callback for that Durang play? Prepare one of the Wacky/Quirky/Odd pieces.

Not only can you use these monologues to audition for a specific role, but you can use them to show your range in general auditions. When asked to prepare two contrasting pieces, you can go beyond simply a comedic and a dramatic (or a contemporary and a classical, if requested), and demonstrate significantly contrasting personas. Put yourself in the director's chair. Which would be more interesting to see an actor perform — a blunt, strong comedic piece with a blunt, strong dramatic piece or a vulnerable comedic piece with an intimidating/dangerous dramatic?

As actors, we must remember that directors are often meeting us for the first time and might assume that we can play only what we show them. So by all means show them! Think of the different impressions you make with your classmates versus coworkers, or on a first date versus a job interview. The pieces you choose tell directors something about you and your capabilities. Sell your strengths, cast yourself against your usual type, and prepare your personal "arsenal" of monologues so you'll be ready for any upcoming audition — no matter what it calls for.

Here are some additional bonuses you'll find in this series:

- The monologues are two minutes and under — some are one minute and under — to fit the time constraints of auditions.

- Very few, if any, of the monologues sound classical. Why? If you are required to do a classical and a contemporary monologue, you want them to contrast as much as possible.

- Only a small number of the monologues require dialects or accents. Why? The rule of thumb is to avoid dialect pieces in auditions unless they are specifically requested. If your accent is not dead-on directors tend to focus on the accent rather than the acting.

- There are 101 monologues to choose from in each book!

- The monologues are from plays as opposed to self-contained pieces. Some of the writers, kindly, at my request, edited the pieces slightly or pasted dialogue so that the monologues would be better suited to audition situations. However, when you read the play, you will see the bulk of the monologue in the same form and that the character and his or her situation have not changed.

- I have included a Tips section in each book containing helpful information that pertains to the selection and preparation of monologues.

I hope you find this new monologue series to be as valuable, time-saving, and innovative as I have set out to make it. In this particular book, I anticipate that you'll find a plethora of monologues to use for upcoming auditions. But don't let that stop you from checking out all of the books in the Audition Arsenal series. I wish you the best of luck in all of your endeavors. And when auditioning, have fun and break a leg!

Janet B. Milstein
www.janetmilstein.com

Tips for Selecting and Preparing a Monologue

Selection

Choose monologues that make you laugh, cry, feel, or think: "I can relate to this!" If a piece speaks to you, even it makes you angry, chances are you will naturally be invested in the piece.

Although each monologue in this book falls into your age range, you should still consider whether you could realistically be cast in this role. If not, choose another piece.

Find a piece that helps you shine. When reading a monologue ask yourself if it really shows what you can do or if it sells you short.

If you are selecting a monologue for a specific role in an upcoming audition, be sure the monologue reveals that you possess the crucial qualities needed to play that role.

If you are preparing for generals and are selecting two or more monologues, choose contrasting pieces that effectively demonstrate your range.

The monologues in this book are two minutes and under. However, you may have auditions that ask for two monologues to be performed in three minutes, or for one-minute monologues. When choosing pieces, make sure they fit the requirements. It is not professional to run overtime. In some cases you may even be timed. Therefore, it is best to keep your monologue at least ten seconds shorter than the allotted time slot. Also, keep in mind when you are reading and timing your monologue(s) that performing time will run longer than reading time.

Pick your monologue(s) now! Don't put it off. Choosing a monologue that fits you well, reading the play, and working and memorizing the piece all take time. If you wait until the last minute, you will not be adequately prepared. Unlike cold readings, monologues give you the chance to show what you're capable of when you have time to prepare a piece.

Preparation

In terms of preparing a monologue for use in auditions, there is much work to be done. Depending on where you are in your process and which methods you are studying, you will work differently. However, I find the following steps to be useful regardless of the method you subscribe to and the extent of your acting experience.

Read the play your monologue is from in its entirety. It will help you to understand the character, history, relationship, setting — everything that is needed even when you only perform the monologue. Not only will it help you to clarify your choices and understand the circumstances, but you just might find a new role, play, or author to add to your list of favorites!

If you have difficulty locating the play, look in the permissions section in the back of the book to contact the author or the author's agent to obtain a copy. If that information becomes outdated, check with Smith and Kraus to see if they can help put you in touch with the right person.

Answer the questions below with respect to your monologue and write your answers in the first person (e.g.: I am twenty-eight, I want her to . . .).

Who are you talking to? Make it very specific, not just "a friend" or "Kate." Use the script for clues about your relationship and fill in the rest.

What is your objective (goal, intention, "fighting for")? It must include the other person. What do you want from him or her? Make it specific and bold — go for your dream goal!

When and where is this taking place? Be very specific as it will inform your environment, your body, and much more.

What happened the moment before the monologue begins? What did the other person say or do that compels you to speak the first line (and the rest of your monologue) right now — not two weeks ago, not yesterday, not an hour ago? The moment before is so important. Test it out and fine-tune it until you have chosen something big enough and personal enough to springboard you into the monologue.

Go through the text of your monologue and with a pencil divide the monologue into beats. Look for the major and minor transitions in the text and use your own system to mark them. Do not skip this step or your monologue will likely be on one note.

How are you going to accomplish your objective — achieve your goal? With tactics or actions. These are the things you do to get what you want. When choosing actions or tactics, put them in the form "to verb" the other person. For example: to beg her, to threaten him, to charm her. Go back to your text, think about your objective, and choose an action/tactic for each beat. Test it out, refine it. The text will help you choose. However, be careful not to be so rigid with this process that your monologue loses spontaneity. Over time, you should change your actions if they get stale.

Personalize your monologue. Are there past events, situations, or other characters mentioned in the text? This is one of the most enjoyable parts of the process — let your imagination run wild and fill in the details that are *not* given in the script (but fall under the given circumstances). Be creative and have fun, but don't stop until you create specifics that will live in you fully.

Memorize your monologue inside out and upside down. I recommend memorizing by rote — quickly and without emotion or expression so as not to get stuck in a line reading. The idea is to drill the lines so well that you never have to be *back in your head* thinking about them when you should be *out in front of you* fighting for your objective from the other person.

Work your monologues with a coach, teacher, director, or fellow actor. Auditioning can be intimidating and what we do when performing alone often changes in the presence of others. You cannot be truly focused on achieving your goal if you are trying to direct yourself at the same time. Work with someone who will be supportive yet honest. No matter where we are in our acting careers, we never stop growing and we all need other people to help guide us.

Acting is a shared experience between performers and audience — even when performing monologues. Remember, you may be auditioning by yourself, but you still have an audience and they're rooting for you.

Hot Tub Haggle
By Werner Trieschmann

Bliss: female, early twenties

Comic

Bliss tries to convince an older neighbor, who is selling a hot tub, to run away with her.

BLISS: I've seen you before you know you used to come into Put a Steak In It that restaurant where I'm the hostess but I'm trying t' get out of there because meat is murder and tastes good but moo cows are pretty and I like fish better but you used to come in there with a woman maybe your wife but you don't anymore and maybe the woman wife is gone . . . and my real name is Imogene but I've changed it to Bliss because of like the karma and it sounds better like Bbblllliiiiissssssss and do ya think you'd want to go with me to some Phish concerts maybe follow them across the country and we could have sex outdoors and recycle and you know whatever . . . I've been told I have an old soul and so I figure I'm at least 300 and I've been around a long time since before there were cars and someday I want to live in a tree 'cause that would be so freakin' awesome you know like oh there's Bliss the Tree Girl did you know she's like 300 years old but don't wander under the tree 'cause she'll pee on you and I would and wouldn't that be just awesome . . .

The Big House
By Barbara Lhota and Ira Brodsky

Elisa: twenty-five years old, a potential guest of *The Big House*

Comic

> *Elisa, a sweet girl from Utah and a big fan of reality TV, has*
> *submitted an audition video for an upcoming reality TV*
> *show that Claire Handal is co-producing. Elisa has been*
> *invited in for an interview. During the interview, Elisa bends*
> *her sweet personality several ways to try to fit into Claire's*
> *vision. In this monologue, Elisa loses all control, winning*
> *her a prime spot on the show.*

ELISA: Call security! Security — Smi — Sma — eerity. *(Confused, try-*
ing to make this work.) Security — Smeerity. Whatever. That's
hard to rhyme. My point is that you aren't the only one who gets
to ask questions. What fears do you have, huh, huh!? How interesting are you? How special?! Is eating perhaps a fear? Does the
sensation of melt-in-your-mouth chocolate send shivers up your
spine? Ooooooohhoooo. *(Jumps out at her.)* Fat — ahhh! That's
a crock! Everybody knows that anyone sick enough to create the
very different — *NOT* — *Big House* reality show is full of neu-
rotic tendencies. Vile, disgusting ideas crowd your head. I see it
now. Yes, control, entrapment, jealousy, boxed potatoes, and
sweaty men playing basketball all summed up by a perky,
patronizing host! I don't want to be on your stupid, hot-headed,
reality rip-off so you can use me until I'm sucked dry and unable
to return to my boring, but pleasant existence. I don't need you,
you Hollywood hack, you pursed-lipped, tight buttocks, Prozac-
treated ninny! I'm better than you. I'm better than all of you!
You can't handle me, Ms. Handal!! *(Beat.)* I've never done that
before. I, I don't know what . . . came over me.

Go See
from *Occupational Hazards*
By Mark McCarthy

Heather: a print model in her late twenties, not stupid, but a little flighty

Comic

A photographer's studio. Heather, a model in her late twenties or early thirties, enters. She is there for an audition, or "go-see." She's late, she's having a terrible day, but she's trying to make the best of it and get through it as professionally as she can.

HEATHER: Hi. Sorry I'm late, it's just that, well I don't want to bore you with a big long story, but the thing is that I would have been on time if it wasn't for one of those you know, things. Are we from the waist up? *(Sits.)* See, I was driving along just as calm as day, trying to decide between the oldies and NPR, thinking to myself, what do you care? It's half of one, six a dozen of the other, and that theme song from . . . *(Almost cries, soldiers on.)* and I just didn't see that little car. Well, truck actually. Cement truck, now that I think about it. Bright yellow cement truck.

Nice tripod.

Anyway, the policeman, who was very nice and really quite attractive, which wasn't helping things at all, keeps making me touch my nose and count backwards — at the same time — and then he says something about failure to yield, and I never really understood yielding anyway, and the not-attractive-at-all truck driver keeps saying something about crazy, and I finally just shouted as loud as I could, "Flipper, all right? It was Flipper!"

And the policeman says, "The TV show?" And the truck driver says, "I love that show!" and tries to imitate the cute little noises the dolphin — porpoise? dolphin always made, but it just sounds like gagging, and I finally said, "My cat Flipper is dead."

And the attractive but stupid policeman doesn't understand what that has to do with anything.

But the thing is I would have seen the bright yellow cement truck just fine, if it hadn't been for the *(She sings.)*, "Flipper! Flipper!" Ready?

(She smiles. She cries.)

Why I Want To Be Your Junior Asia Miss
By Lauren D. Yee

Bekki Lee Kim: Female. Early to mid-twenties. A perky, slightly
vapid girl who means well.

Comic

*It's Bekki Lee Kim's turn to speak at the Junior Asia Miss
Pageant. She stands on stage, decked in her finest for the
"scholarship competition."*

BEKKI: My name is Bekki Lee Kim and I want to be your next Junior
Asia Miss! That's spelled B-E-K-K-I with an *i* and two *k*'s. *(Making bad pun.)* 'Cause *I* want to be your next Junior Asia Miss,
OK? *(Waits for audience laughter — there is none.)* All right!
Time for the questions. Super! *(Looks for questions — finally
sees teleprompter.)* There they are! All right! "Why do you want
to be the next Junior Asia Miss?" Well . . . umm . . . I do have a
reason . . . can we get back to that? Wait! *(Turns to crib notes
on her arm, reads.)* Because I believe Asia is a very special place
with many people who are also Asian. All right then! "What
would you do if you became the next Junior Asia Miss?" Do?
You mean, *who* would I do? *(Waits, sees more on teleprompter.)*
Oh, there's more. "How would you be a positive role model for
young girls?" A model? I would love to be a model! I think it's
very important that if you're a model, you be a positive one, too.
Any kind of model would be fine with me. Shoe modeling, hair
modeling, hand modeling . . . *(Beat.)* What's so funny . . . ? OK,
I'm not a genius. I can't explain Kepler's laws for all the tea in
China. I don't even know how much tea is "all the tea in China!"
I'm no Edgar Einstein, but it's unfair of you to assume I'm here
because I'm young and beautiful and the ugly girls aren't because
they're young and ugly. Because this scholarship competition is
not about looks! — it's about . . . well, it's not about looks! It's
about being Asian. And about being proud of it and doing something positive. I may not know *(Pronounces incorrectly.)* chem-
mistry or psy-koology or physololerogy, but whatever I do does

a lot more than those smart people who know everything and do nothing. That's why I should be your Junior Asia Miss — because I'll try. And that's what makes Asia a very special country. *(Triumphant, about to exit, then trips on skirt.)*

The Gary Chain
By Adam Simon

Tricia: mid-twenties, airport newsstand employee

Seriocomic

The play is a whirlwind tour of what happens in three lives after a brief celebrity encounter at an airport in Gary, Indiana. Tricia works in the airport and delivers the following to a co-worker during an early morning smoke break. After a discussion of the sad state of their love lives, her co-worker has just bluntly asked Tricia "When was the last time you even had sex?"

TRICIA: Somebody told me — or maybe it was in a movie — I don't know. Anyway, they said "the thing about sex is that it's impossible to replicate" and that struck me as wrong. Sometimes things, ideas usually strike me as really horribly wrong. I think that some things like "sex is impossible to replicate" are so wrong that I get ill. I have to take a moment to reason it out with the voice in my head who does its best to temper the one sided argument. And I'll say that that's a load of shit, sex is entirely possible to replicate, it's biologically simple, it can happen the same way again and again and it (the voice) will say that it's had sex with the same woman hundreds of times (it's a wife I assume, sometimes I give the voice a wife . . . *(Realizing for the first time.)* and a gender I guess) and of those hundreds of times it's never truly been the same. Now I don't think that can be true and I'll say "Yeah, but aren't you divorced?" Cause I invented the voice, and I invented its wife and I can take her away, it's my right. And it'll say "Are you saying that if we had found a way to replicate sex we wouldn't be divorced?" The voice argues me into corners sometimes, but I think that's true. I think marriages work when sex is replicated into everything and not in a photocopy facsimile way but in a conch-shell-held-to-my-ear-sounds-like-the-ocean way — meaning I can take the ocean to the dry cleaners, to work, to the doctor's, I could even take the ocean to the beach. I think that in a successful marriage sex can be replicated into a ten-second cell phone conversation about what's for dinner. And that's — "sex can't be replicated" — that's how far it usually takes me to understand why things disagree with me so much. My husband says I shouldn't let things get under my skin so much. And I don't say it out loud, but I think he doesn't let enough get under his skin.

Bridge Partners
By Ira Brodsky and Barbara Lhota

Cindy: late twenties, a former rock-and-roll singer

Seriocomic

> *After a series of love-life and career setbacks, two women,*
> *both who went to the same high school, accidentally meet*
> *up on the Benjamin Franklin Bridge in Philadelphia. Coin-*
> *cidently, both of them have come to kill themselves by jump-*
> *ing off the bridge. Cindy, who was a wild-child with*
> *rock-and-roll ambitions, is happy to pour her heart out to*
> *her former schoolmate Susan. Susan's competitive nature*
> *forces her into a battle with Cindy over who has had to bear*
> *more of life's miseries.*

CINDY: I said, very meditatively like, love will find me at the right time. I put myself in the hands of the Great Creator. It's been a real struggle. Every time I pass a club and hear the music, I want to go in and see what's cookin'. Or I'd be surfin' the Internet and start reading the personal ads. But I stopped myself. No, no, I said. You have put yourself in the hands of the Great Creator. I go to work at Tower Records, and I stock the CDs of all the other rock-and-roll divas and that kinda bums me out. But anyway. I'm accepting of life. I neither pull nor push. I let the tide carry me. *(Singing.)* "The tide is high, but I'm holdin' on. I'm gonna be your Number one. Number one." Anyway this has been my life for the past two months. Solitary, OK lonely, well, downright boring. And that's when Seth walks into Tower. So I'm straightening the oldies section. Seth is tall, cute, intelligent, discerning — everything you want in a record buyer. And he smiles at me. Notice — *he* smiles first. I'm not pushing or pullin'. I'm going with the flow. I smile back. Small talk. Blah, blah, blah. He asks me on a date. What was wrong I thought? There must be something wrong with him to ask me on a date. He was celibate. He had sworn off sex. My guess is that he figured I wouldn't be much of a temptation. He even asked me to be his celibate wife. I am a failure in my art, a failure in life and love. Just a complete failure. I suppose it could be worse. For instance, if I were diagnosed with a disfiguring and fatal ailment. But I guess God thought that would be redundant.

Skid Marks: A Play About Driving
By Lindsay Price

Jillian: twenty-one. Jillian is a high-strung girl who sees her car as a person.

Comic

Jillian lectures her car on its recent unsatisfactory behavior. She believes "Herman" has been acting up on purpose.

JILLIAN: Herman, I want you to listen up and listen good. You're going to start properly. You're not going to stall. You're not going to make those knock, knock, cha-ping noises like last time. I know you were just doing it to spite me cause I took you to the mechanic and the mechanic said there was nothing wrong! So there's no point in making knock, knock, cha-ping noises. I'm on to you now. I know the little game you're trying to play. You'd best remember who's in charge. Who's got the keys Herman? Who's got the keys? I could put you in a no-park zone, let you get towed and never collect you. How'd you like that huh? I could take you to the wrong side of town and leave you all alone with the windows down and the keys in the ignition. That wouldn't be nice would it? Would it? So no more knock, knock, cha-ping noises. No more chugha-choughing. No more wheeza, wheeza, humpa humpa znack znack znack when we're going up hills. And absolutely no more spitting gas when I'm filling the tank. I can hear you snickering, Herman, when I'm standing there covered in gas but let me tell you it is so not funny. Not funny. Repeat after me please. I will not spit gas on Jillian when she is trying to fill the tank. *(She listens.)* Don't mumble! *(She listens.)* Thank you. There. I'm glad we had this little talk. I hope we can improve our relationship and put this little difficulty behind us. All right. Let's drive.

I Think You Think I Love You
By Kelly Younger

Branwyn: twenties, female, frantic talker, highly caffeinated

Comic

> *Branwyn has just returned from a long hike on Castle Rock*
> *where she spread the ashes of her recently deceased mother.*
> *She is relaying the absurd story to a stranger named Mark*
> *whom she believes is interested in buying her mother's*
> *house. Here, Branwyn shares what she thinks is the most*
> *humiliating part of her day before she discovers Mark has*
> *actually arrived for a blind date that slipped her mind.*

BRANWYN: I take out Mom's ashes. I recite a line from Shakespeare, *Othello,* she liked that play. And then I said, good-bye Mom, and tossed her ashes up in the air. And by air, of course, I mean wind, and by wind I mean the wind blowing in the direction I'm standing and I'm sorry, but I never paid much attention to those old sailor movies that say never spit into the wind because sure enough Mom blows right out and back at me. And by back at me, of course, I mean my face and by my face I mean my nose and mouth. So of course my face is all wet and weepy so Mom sticks to my face, and I freak out and inhale with horror and down she goes. Not all of it, or her, but enough, you know? Just a bit to be absolutely horrified that I've just inhaled some of my mother, which I'm sure could be some beautiful metaphor for Mom living inside me and all that sentimental stuff but really all I can think is my mother tastes like charcoal. Not that I know, but you can imagine, you know? So I start pouring water out of my canteen onto my face and into my mouth and nose and I'm stumbling all around the top of Castle Rock thinking I'm either going straight to hell for cannibalizing my mother or I'm going straight off the side of this rock like that old Indian girl who couldn't live without her lover. It's OK, you can laugh.

The Whiz
By Ira Brodsky and Barbara Lhota

Donna: twenty-four, mousy, a therapy patient

Comic

> *After much anguish, Donna, a shy and unhappy young woman, goes to see a psychologist. However, when she enters the waiting room, she is accosted by Hettie, a flaky patient, who pretends to be Dr. Gold and wants to help Donna get started immediately on her therapy. Despite Hettie's odd behavior, she actually manages to help Donna through one of her phobias, before her trick is revealed.*

DONNA: Call it quits? I'm just getting started. I have things to talk about, sister. I've got a backlog of pain and sorrow and anger that I've been itching to get out. Roar! This thing with Howard is nothin'. I've got issues, Dr. Gold. Do you hear me — is-sues! My parents died when I was an infant, and I was raised by an aunt and uncle. And sure they meant well, but they were busy running a large roadside farm stand and didn't have time for me. And then ever since that huge storm back in, I don't know, '92 when I was about twelve — nothing's ever been quite right. I mean I have these dreams all the time — midgets, and witches, flying monkeys, for God's sake! And sometimes I feel so empty inside. That's why I think nobody loves me. I mean, sometimes I think, I think my head is full of stuffing, and you already saw how timid I am. I'm a coward. I know it. But could it be that something's really missing *(She bangs on her chest.)* in here? Am I heartless? Do I literally, lack a heart? Is that why no one loves me? You tell me, doctor. You have to help me! I can't go on like this!

The Dead Deportee
By Dan O'Brien

Meg: twenties

Comic

> *Meg, a Ph.D. candidate in women's studies, explains to her roommates just how her identical twin sister Mug became brain-damaged, and why she's kept Mug's existence a secret for so long.*

MEG: Well, you see, it went like this: I was the first one out of my mother's womb by at least ten seconds or so. You know how I like to get places early. Anyway — all this is according to my mother, by the way, who was an eyewitness, naturally — I came out of my mother's womb and seemed pretty happy with the world. Pretty content. But when I saw that there was this other baby coming out right after me — my sister, Mug — I got really very jealous. And I reached in with my baby fists and I grabbed hold of that umbilical cord — hers, not mine — and I . . . well, I began to yank. To twist. To squeeze . . . And the doctor and the nurses couldn't disentangle me, my grip was so ferocious. I yanked and pulled and twisted that cord around my little sister's little neck, and by the time they'd thought to use a very low-voltage electric shock to stop my heart for a second or two to loosen my grip, my twin sister Mug had suffered severe oxygen deprivation to the brain. *(Beat.)*

> I gave my twin sister brain damage . . .
> At least that's what they tell me.

La Llorona and Other Tales of the American Southwest
By Elise Forier

Monica: twenties, a Latina single mother, with a one-year-old child; she has just learned she is pregnant again.

Dramatic

> *Southwestern Arizona. The present. Monica's welfare benefits are going to be cut. Her Aunt Tia is dying of cancer, and if Monica gets a job, there will be no one to care for the sick woman. She is speaking to her younger cousin Esmeralda, who has been taking advanced placement classes at night and has been unable to help Monica or their aunt.*

MONICA: You fucking bitch! What is this crap about summer school? You think I don't know what you're up to? Go to school so you don't have to deal with the shit around here? A little extra special school for extra special Esmeralda. Vendida bitch! I'm losing the government checks. Two months, no benefits, where am I gonna work, eh? I got to take care of Tia, I got to take care of the baby; am I gonna work the graveyard shift, maybe? And how do I get there? Walk? All the jobs I qualify for are jobs for assholes. Sweep this. Count that. Fit this little plastic part into that little plastic part. And can I ask you to be here for me? For Tia? No. You are la flora blanca, la chica perfecta — leave her alone, she's got to do Calculus. Not everyone can be perfect like you. Do you think I wanted this? I just wanted to feel safe. You see a whore when you look at me, but let me tell you Esme — a man making love to you is yours. In the world, he goes out in cars, he's got a job, he's got shit to do. But if he's inside you, he ain't going nowhere, as long as it lasts. That's what I want. That's what I want. I just want him to stay. Every time they do me, I think "maybe this time he'll stay." Esme. Tia is dying and I am all alone in this house with it. Help me. Can you help me, please?

A Good Solid Home
By Barbara Lhota and Janet B. Milstein

Angie: young adult, a New Jersey girl

Dramatic

> *Angie gave up her baby a few months back. Suddenly, she gets the urge to know that her son, Ricky, is in good hands. She takes a trip across several states to check out her son's new home. In this piece, Angie begs for the opportunity to just take one last look around before she says good-bye for good.*

ANGIE: I'm not asking you to *engage* in anything! I just want to talk. I just want to talk about things, ya know. And I don't care if it's a good time. I just drove from Jersey City for God's sake. Twenty-four hours in a beat-up Sedan with a chain-smoker and no air. So I don't care if it's the perfect timin', I need to talk today. And I'm not doin' any maneuverin' or I woulda brought a lawyer myself. Right? Right?! *(Beat.)* I'd be pretty stupid — totally stupid to drive all the way here and start tryin' to maneuver with you guys. You're college educated and all. I don't even have a high school diploma. I guess I've just been real sad. Like there's a hole in the middle of my gut since I gave him away that day. I always had sort of a hole in me, but it's bigger now and more noticeable. Even my boyfriend noticed it first thing when he came home. I told him I was pregnant and gave the baby away. He was like, "That's so strange cause I could see there was a hole in you. It's so obvious." I know you don't think I've done anything in my life. I haven't. I guess, havin' Ricky made me feel like I did somethin' so good, I wanted to hold onto it. *(Pause.)* A kid makes you feel like ya did somethin'. Like you accomplished somethin'. I know I ain't got a lot to give him like you do. I mean, you live so close to Disney World for one. And you're both real smart and nice. Even when you use big words. I just kinda wanted to see the place. Ya know? Check it out. Make sure it looked right. I get afraid some times. I get afraid that I won't have another chance. *(Beat.)* Anyway, *(Looking out the window.)* I gotta go get Tommy, my boyfriend. He's sleepin'. He told me he'd whip my butt if I didn't get him outta the sun, so he don't burn up like a lobster. *(Pause.)* So I ain't ever gonna see my son again, am I?

IceSPEAK
By Jeanette D. Farr

Bee-Bee: twenties to thirties, a tough broad who wants to be a rock star, not afraid to speak her mind, but vulnerable

Dramatic

> *Bee-Bee will do anything to be a rock star. After one of her sets in a local dive bar, she brings home Charlie, a local man who asks her to play one of her songs for him. She shares that being smart generally comes with a cost.*

BEE-BEE: Before my daddy passed on, he looked me in the eye and told me the only man I would get to love me would be just like him. *(Pause.)* I think that really fucked me up, you know? He wasn't all that bad — didn't touch me or nothin', but liked to pick my brain a little too much. He wanted me to be smarter than him for whatever the reason. When he would start in with the lessons, I would make up songs in my head. It was the only way I knew to . . . to really tell him what I felt . . . those songs in my head. He would get so pissed 'cause he always thought I was daydreaming. But in fact . . . I was trying to speak to him. "Rebecca!" He'd say, "WAKE UP!" with some gesture that would get my attention. He started off as Dr. Seuss then turned into Nietzsche. A little fucking hard to handle at five, you know? *(With incredible urgency.)* You promise me something, Charlie. Promise me you won't pick my brain too much. I'm not gonna let that happen to me — not again, got it? You want something from me and me from you — that's all. But you're not going to teach me anything I don't already know. Nothing against you. But the music I play — It's for me. Nobody else. And I'm gonna play that song for you — but only 'cause I want to. That clear? You gotta promise me that. Will ya? Will ya, Charlie? *(Pause.)* I've left you speechless. It's your turn. What's your story, Charlie? You have a father you're ashamed of?

Not Everyone Sees It
By Barbara Lhota and Ira Brodsky

Margo: young adult

Dramatic

> *Margo's parents have been concerned about her mental health since she attempted suicide and they had her temporarily committed. When Margo was released, she felt angrier than ever and decided to run away to Chicago. Before she leaves, she goes to visit an old friend to explain what has been going on in her life.*

MARGO: I got on the Web, and I just happened on this encyclopedia of suicides. I mean, that someone would bother to look up all the dates of the important people who committed suicide and type them up and make a Web page. I wondered who that person was. A lot of people have done it — killed themselves. Anyway, I started reading my Nietzsche book, that same quote, "That which does not kill me makes me stronger." Usually it makes me feel better, but it didn't this time. And then I started thinking of all those sappy quotes people put on inspirational posters. Those posters with whales flying out of the water and people climbing huge mountain cliffs: "A journey of a thousand miles begins with a single step" and "No man is an Island." And in my head, the sayings just kept filling my brain and they started attacking one another like a bunch of wild tigers ripping to shreds the other quotes. Words were flying all over the place and poking into each other. *(Laughs sadly.)* And then I thought of this old quote. I think it's Aristotle or Confucius. "Everything has beauty, but not everyone sees it." It made me sad. Because I don't think I see beauty in anything anymore.

Sueño
By Scott McMorrow

G-Girl: twenty, a latina gang leader in San Francisco's Mission District

Dramatic

> *G-Girl rules her world as a gang leader in San Francisco's Mission District. This hard-core female gangster learns that being more ruthless than her male counterparts isn't the only thing that will keep her on top. In this scene, G-Girl is talking to her homeless, long-estranged mother (Lorna), explaining that life in the gangs is good, and that life on the streets is better due to G-Girl's gang leadership.*

G-GIRL: Shit is better with me in charge. You see me now? I ain't the little girl you walked out on. My juice is the stuff keepin' it rollin'. Remember what it was like before? Seemed every day one of us was getting popped in the street by them fucks. Daddy went down that way. Now I know he was good. Hard, but fair. And look where that shit got him. Dead. That's what. I don't give a fuck who think they badder than me. No. I can deal with them. What shakes me is the one's that don't know no better. Go around with they heads in the sky thinking they gonna be something like me. Hell no. I say, thems the ones gotta go, and fast. See, the bad asses you can control, give 'em work, put 'em on your payroll and keep 'em close. Them others, they causin' trouble by stepping too close to you without letting on. They sneaky like that, little rats. Sneaky like you, jumpin' up after all these years with your momma bullshit. Where the fuck you been? A little girl need her momma's love. You ain't give me that. You ain't give me jack. But I can hang. You wanna call me daughter, fine. But I tell you something. I don't give a fuck who you be. I ain't callin' you mother, 'cause she dead. You might be her, but what the fuck that mean? Everybody got a mother. Nothing special there.

A Story About a Girl
By Jacquelyn Reingold

Denise: twenties, tough and loud

Seriocomic

> *Denise gets fired from her fast-food restaurant job for stand-ing up for Jessica, a co-worker who doesn't talk. They both walk out, and head across the street for Chinese food. Here Denise tells Jessica about herself, which launches a friend-ship.*

DENISE: I don't mind, I hated working there. I was kind of primed to lose that job. Did you read *Fast Food Nation? (Jessica shakes her head no.)* I got it yesterday and I was reading it before I went to sleep, well, you will not believe what goes into those restaurants. The history, the implications, the politics, the cows. The guy who wrote that book, he knows how to use his words. No offense, OK? Do you talk? What is it with you and talking or not talking anyway? You want to write it down or something? *(Jessica writes something on the place mat. Denise reads it:)* Deli-cate. OK. Whatever. You ever see *The Miracle Worker?* With Patty Duke? *(Jessica shakes her head no.)* Anyway, I can talk enough for two. You should come see me perform. I'm a perfor-mance artist actress poet writer singer standup and generally opinionated loud-mouthed kind of big girl. I been thru it all, you know. I been abused, beat up, addicted, I was born with ADD ADHD dyslexic synthetic rejected inspected you name it I got it. My stepfathers abused me in ways I don't need to go into. I have concluded the only way for me to get through this here life with this body and these emotions is to keep my mouth open and say what I'm thinking. Cause I aim to make things righter. That's how I see why I'm on this earth. I think we make a good pair. Don't you? I could use a friend that knows how to listen and not trying all the time to shut me up. Cause I won't be shut up. *You all hear that??* You can't shut me up. You can lock me up beat me up mess me up or fuck me up, but you can't shut Denise Johnson up.

Four Glasses
By Marki Shalloe

France: twenties

Dramatic

> *France lives with her mother, a schizophrenic who is increasingly unable to live a normal life; the mother's situation has become even more precarious as France's father has gone off with another woman. France needs her mother to understand that France cannot take care of her. She can't bear to witness the increasing mental illness in her mother that she fears she has inherited. France has begun to believe that her only escape lies in drinking.*

FRANCE: YOU went out trying to find a job, Mama; YOU got us on public assistance.

YOU learned how to drive and bought the groceries and cooked them, which — even if you were lousy at it — is better than Daddy ever did.

But you never complained, did you?

You never let him in on the little secret that you're not addled because of his mean mouth and his inability to keep his dick in his pants,

you're not "eccentric,"

you're SCHIZOPHRENIC and pieces of your mind are tearing off on a daily basis and

you can no longer take care of yourself.

No, you just cried.

Don't look at me like it's my job to take care of you.

It was your job to ask him, not weep and pack him a damn lunch as he ran away.

You have no savior, Mama, but I do. I have whiskey.

My Redeemer is secure . . . it doesn't have a breakdown because it has to do something normal, like make fruitcakes for Christmas; it doesn't see things that aren't there.

It doesn't remind me with every look what I'm gonna turn into.

A while with My Savior Jim Beam and I don't care if adults commit adultery and I don't covet other daughters who have no worries because their parents are normal and they are too.

There it is, Mama. The first and most important glass.

The first drink taken in pain and sorrow and self-hatred and with the deep sip of realization that I am *damaged*.

That the tiny flaw you have passed down through your DNA will get bigger and bigger until I'm crushing fruitcakes with Sylvester the Cat tumblers and shitting in a container I hand to other people.

So now do you understand?

The ONLY thing that will kill it is alcohol.

Threnody
By David-Matthew Barnes

Dana: early twenties

Dramatic

> *Dana is trapped in a volatile relationship. She is also
> heavily addicted to speed. After being up for three days, she
> confronts her boyfriend about a night when his love for her
> turned brutal and violent.*

DANA: The orchard, Jake. Do you remember that night? I just remember the dirt. I was laying there in the dirt . . . you were on me
and you kept pushing against me. Your fingers felt like razors,
tearing at me. I could smell the booze on your breath and it was
so sour and it made me gag. I wanted to vomit, but I was choking on the dirt. The fucking dirt was in my mouth. And I
couldn't breathe. I was fighting you. I was begging you to stop.
But you wanted to come. *(Beat.)* And I let you have your way.
(Beat.) Then you left me there, in the orchard, in the dark . . . so
I followed you, back inside. Back to that graduation party where
you told all of your friends to be polite to me. I wanted to claw
my way out of that place. I would have dug a tunnel with my
bare hands just to get away from you and those people. I was
standing in the corner and I was staring at the wall and the music
was pounding in my ear. I wanted to reach up and grab this baby
blue streamer and tie it around my neck. And choke. Their eyes
and their red plastic cups filled with beer and strawberry wine
and ice cubes. I just stood there. And I was freezing, and all of
their eyes were on me. My dress was ripped. And I looked down,
to try and fix it. And I saw the blood, Jake. It was running down
my legs . . . like my soul was crying. They knew what you had
done to me. Even though I told you no. Do you realize that,
Jake? I kept saying no! But you couldn't hear me, because I was
full of dirt. You were so messed up that night. I had to drive us
home . . . and I was still bleeding. From your scratches and scars.
I brought us back here so you could pass out and so that I could
wash the dirt out of my hair. And that smell . . . that awful,
awful smell of you and their judgment. I can still smell it sometimes.

Pensacola
By David-Matthew Barnes

Marie: young adult

Comic

> *On her first date with a Cuban pizza-delivery man, an exu-*
> *berant, fantastical, and very Southern Marie confesses her*
> *strategy to become the next Miss Florida.*

MARIE: I've been studying all night to become Miss Florida. I just never realized it until just recently that this is my calling. Now, let me tell you what I found in my studies. I didn't care much for Miss Jamie Lynn Bolding. She won way back in 1996 and her talent was lyrical ballet. How tacky. But I simply died when I discovered Miss Kristin Alicia Beall Ludecke. She was Miss Florida five thousand years ago in 1995 — and she was wonderful. Very classy and elegant. Her platform issue was self-esteem through music and the arts and then she sang opera. It was something foreign and breathtaking. Sort of like *you*. And I just loved Miss Jennifer DelGallo. Now she was Miss *Pensacola* in 1996 and she sang the hell out of *(She actually sings this, very operatic:)* "Don't Rain on My Parade!" I swear to you when I read about this, the hair on my scalp stood up when I imagined her performing. I was beside myself. I nearly peed my pants. And her platform issue was the value of the family. Couldn't you just die? She was so brave in those democratic times. I'm gonna write to her, a belated letter of support. And I'll tell her about my plans. Maybe I'll even take her to lunch. Some place healthy and *Christian*. Up until last night, around midnight, I wanted to go to secretary school. But now, I have opted for a more glamorous and socially fulfilling career choice. *(She stands on the sofa and looks out at an imaginary crowd.)* I'm gonna become Miss Florida and feed starving children in Third-World countries. It came to me in a dream, a vision I had last night. I saw myself, in a bathing suit with cute polka dots. I was wearing a tiara and a sash and I was surrounded by hungry children. And I was feeding them *pizza* and they all loved me. And the President of the United States of

America was there and he shook my hand and he said to me, "Miss Florida, Miss Marie Baker, you have changed the world." I smiled. *(She does.)* I waved. *(She does.)* I even cried. *(She starts to and stops.)* There was a video crew there and they shot the whole thing and in my dream it was being sold on television for only $19.95. So, as an American girl, I feel compelled to make my dreams come true. *(Pause.)* I just haven't told Mama yet.

Shattered
By Lindsay Price

Hannah: teetering on the fence between childhood and adulthood. She's a lower-class romantic who works as a secretary. Twenty.

Dramatic

Hannah sits on the beach in the middle of the night, drinking from a bottle of scotch. She's just found out she's pregnant. In the play, there are seven versions of Hannah at different ages. In this monologue Hannah at twenty talks to Hannah at seventy.

HANNAH: You should come and sit over here. I've managed to carve out the exact spot where the water comes up over my toes. Come on. I'm celebrating. I just got off the phone with the doctor an hour ago. I got off the phone, went straight to the liquor store and kept on walking till I ended up here. I can't go home. I can't go to the office. I can't tell my mother, I can't tell John. John. John. John. Mr. Roberts. Can I get you some more coffee Mr. Roberts? Mail is on your Roberts Mr. Desk! Roberts. Did you know people used to think that if a girl had a very hot bath and drank castor oil at the same time the baby inside her would disappear? Just like that. Poof, disappear. Wouldn't that be great? One hot bath, and poof. John's baby. John's big old baby. My boss' baby. John Philip Arthur Roberts. I have never met anyone with two middle names before. I'm supposed to call him John. Mr. Roberts in the office but outside the office I'm supposed to call him John. Like we're close or something. He's really good looking. He has almost purple eyes. I've never known anyone with almost purple eyes before. *(She sighs.)* I want to bury myself in the sand and drink scotch. Maybe it will work. Maybe the baby will disappear.

Knock
By Lauren Kettler

Miranda: in her early twenties. She is, as she mentions, blind. A touch of the Southern belle makes her seem almost fragile, a handicap she'd kill to overcome.

Seriocomic

> *The action takes place in a semi-decent motel room some-where in Key West. Miranda is down from Tallahassee for the weekend with boyfriend Lem. When a despondent Lem apparently shoots himself, Miranda takes refuge in Joy's room next door. Thus begins the unlikely bonding of two very different women, both in the throes of facing their respective fears. As the monologue begins, Miranda is still coming to terms with the evening's shocking events*

MIRANDA: You know the worst part? Somewhere inside me I feel almost giddy. I do. Not because Lem is, you know . . . gone. Not because of that. It's just there's this other part of me, the part that's been unsure for as long as I've known that boy whether he's the one I really want. Which is OK, right? I mean, you don't have to go and marry every guy you hook up with, do you? I just got it in my fool head that there's someone else out there for me. Someone who won't care that I'm blind, who'll love me anyway, just like Lem. Only, I'll love him back without an ounce of reservation. I won't be worrying all the time about having my freedom. And I won't be getting mad at him either every time he says he loves me. Or asks me to be his wife, and makes all kinds of plans around it, like getting ourselves married on some crazy old boat out there on the third largest barrier reef in the world. The very first time he asks me, I'll tell him yes, without one hesitation. So he won't be asking me a million times a day, or doing anything really stupid like proposing on the scoreboard at half-time at a Seminoles football game. Or shooting himself in the head. This time it'd be different. Because I'd know it's right. In my heart I'd know it. Wouldn't that be something? You know, when you can't see, there's a whole universe the seeing world doesn't even know about. It's like your imagination has full run of your mind, if you know what I mean. And I can see him. I don't know what he looks like, but I can see the dumb bastard. I just don't know how the heck to find him, that's all.

Black Flamingos
By Julius Galacki

EV: "I'm not crazy, Toby. I just got one extra voice in my head." Mid-twenties to early thirties. A child-woman, who maintains a disarming innocence; she is physically identical to Cecilia, however her hair is uncombed and she wears soiled clothing — like an untended little girl.

Seriocomic

Ev, short for Evangeline, lives with Isaac in the middle of nowhere in an abandoned gas station. Tobias' car has broken down nearby and he has walked over for help. Instead, Isaac has drugged him and then tied him to a rock out in the hot sun. In this scene, Ev has already explained to Tobias that Isaac is a demon and will most certainly kill Tobias when he returns. She'd like to go free herself, but can't so she certainly couldn't help him. Now, desperate, Toby lies by responding positively to her previously stated romantic interest in him: "And when I'm your husband, don't you want him — me — to live?"

EV: Very much, I want you to be my husband, Tobias. You see, you know who, he's impotent. Demons are always impotent. That's why they want to kill. A long time ago, God cut off their penises and then promised to give them back only if they did his bidding. But God lied. He wouldn't give them back. It's population control, see, demons live forever. He wanted more people than demons on this earth, 'cause God likes to see people die. It's all about a harmony in his head. So, demons kill as many people as they can — on the road, in the air, coming out of tubs. Demons are everywhere, dickless and pissed off. And that makes God happy.

home
By Heather Taylor

Cil: twenty-three

Dramatic

Cil left home at eighteen and swore never to return. In hopes to save up money to make a big move to South America, she goes back and finds herself slipping back into the familiar patterns of home. This monologue ends the play. Cil is at the worktable at the factory surrounded by piles of basins, etc. She is speaking to Tracy, a new worker. As Cil goes through the instructions of how to polish basins, she does what she is saying with ease. In the end she leaves the audience with the question — will she ever leave?

CIL: It's easy, ya know? Tracy it's Tracy, right? All ya do is take the brush and do a quick clean. Then polish. Wipe it down. Then put 'em there. You'll get the hang of it. *(Silence.)* You know in South America, there's these places that are just fields of salt. You can walk clean across the whole thing and it's like this big desert and it feels like your footprints are the first ones that have ever touched that place. The winds just blow over after and they disappear ya know? Manda, that's my sister, she thinks it's the same thing as those blizzards that sweep in sometimes but it's not. The whole place is different — like it's gentle and quiet with these parts — they're just all green and lush and wild. And families let you come right in — I mean you could just eat a meal with them and everything even though they ain't got much to give. Not like that would happen here. *(Pause.)* I'm savin' up ya know. It won't be too long then I'll head down. Think Manda's gonna come too. I mean she's at college and all that but when I'm gone she's gonna come back here and save up. She'll get my job when I leave — just wanted to let you know. Just in case you thought you'd get to move up and all that. But if you work hard, you could always get it after she goes . . . not too much longer. Oh and you'd like her. She's great. It's so weird, always thought she's just a kid but she's not ya know. She really isn't. A friend maybe. She could be a great friend. *(Pause.)* Ya know, it's gonna be great down there in South America — and I've been practicing. Got the tape right here. *(Cil shows the tape player in her pocket.)* No one minds really. Just listen to it in one ear anyway. But I've been around for awhile, ya know, so don't think you can do it too. Got one for Manda for her birthday — I don't want to be the only one who can speak down there. God it's gonna be great . . . and the coolest thing is you can hear monkeys chattering in the jungles and you can sleep on the edge of it on the sand between the palm trees and the ocean and feel completely safe. Just you and the ocean. Just you and the ocean, ya know? It'll be just me and Manda and the ocean.

Mud People
By Keith Huff

Barb: twenties to thirties

Seriocomic

*Barb is an emotionally scarred woman with a young daugh-
ter, the product of an incestuous relationship. In this scene,
she speaks to Clay Radley, a milk-truck driver who is very
much in love with her and proposes every time he stops by
the diner owned by Barb's family. Barb is obviously lying
through her teeth in this scene. But her lies go beyond sub-
terfuge: She becomes almost childlike in her presentation —
the fallout of years of abuse and emotional mistrust.*

BARB: My husband's name is Adam. Adam's a better man than you'll
ever be. He's got morals and clean fingernails and shaves every
day. Not just in-between milk loads. He's a lawyer in Hurley.
And he's contemplating running for public office some day. He's
got aspirations more than a tooth-picking gear-grinder and he
don't smell like one, neither. Adam's decent. I tell him something's X-Y-Z he believes me: X-Y-Z. He don't go sucking up the
cheap gossip drool from out between the planks-a tavern floors
around Claybourne Rising and taking that over the worda the
girl give her heart to him. Fact is, he was by Tuesday last in a real
car close to the ground with four doors to ask me how'd I'd like
living in a house by the lake with a pier. Soon's the arrange-
ments're made we're setting the day. So, Clay Radley, you can
quit oozing your romantic snake-oil charms on an involved
woman. He ain't pluck-bald on the top for one. He ain't bow-
legged for another. And he don't smoke or drink beer for a third
thing 'cause he knows it's bad for you. His hair's got this black
raven smooth quality what looks almost purple in the moonlight
dark. Plus he's got crystal blue–sky eyes you look into what
sometime tell the future. They ain't yellow and bloodshot and
tell you nothing but what he been drinking last night or how
long he's been driving. And his mustache . . . it's a lot like his
hair only it's got little flecks-a gray. Not 'cause Adam's old.
Mostly 'cause he's distinguished looking like he's been eating
powder sugar donuts and forgot to wipe his mouth.

Groom and Doom
By Douglas Hill

Emmie: eighteen to twenty-two, Mama's angel and a bride-to-be, seemingly innocent girl from southeast Oklahoma

Seriocomic

> *Afraid of making a mistake, Emmie has run from her own wedding to the basement of the church. Her mother, Ann, and her maid of honor, Joanna, have followed her down there. Emmie's nerves about getting married are only agitated by her conservative mother's firm belief that Emmie can do no wrong and would never make a mistake.*

EMMIE: Mom, you can't say those things about me anymore! It's too much! *(Pause.)* About a year ago . . . Joanna and I . . . were drinking. And *we . . . No — I* was drunk. *I* did it. *I* was curious. And I . . . was curious . . . about her. And there's more, but I don't know how much I can tell you. *(Pause.)* We tried pot later. *(Under Ann's glare, she offers:)* And there was a week when I thought I was late. And I thought about eloping because the wedding was still four months off and I didn't want you to know. And I didn't want a maternity wedding dress. I've been listening to rap music in the car . . . *(Pause.)*

   I don't want to disappoint you, so that's why I never said anything. Because I love you. But you can't keep calling me "angel." It's too hard on me. And with all the fuckups in the past year and you thinking — *(Ann starts to react.)* No — that's how I talk, Mom. For real. With all the fuckups in the past year and you thinking I was better than I am . . . I was afraid you'd find out that I wasn't quite so good. And then you'd hate me. And it's stupid, I know, but . . . I thought it was better to just keep you in the dark. *(Pause.)* So . . . do . . . do you hate me?

Kim and Claudia Capture Death in a Box
By Lauren D. Yee

Kim: female, early to late twenties. A young woman with a mental disorder that has given her the intellect of a child — she is slow not stupid.

Seriocomic

Kim speaks to Death, whom she and her protective older sister Claudia have captured in a box. Death has been coaxing her to let him out.

KIM: I know what you want. You want me to let you out so you can take me away. Claudia says you can't trust Death, even if he's in a box. I may be slow up here, but that doesn't mean I don't understand things. Claudia says I'm like everyone else, just I take my time. And I am going to take all my time with you. Claudia says I could be on *Jeopardy* some day. I just need to know things. I have a big box of cards on my second-to-top shelf and I study them before I go to bed so I can know things. Claudia says if I let you out, I won't get to be on *Jeopardy*. Claudia says if I let you out, I won't get to do a lot of things. *(Creepy voice.)* "Dead men tell no tales." And I'm going to do a lot of things. As long as I have you here, Claudia says I won't have to worry about getting sick or falling off my bed because you can't come to get me. So many things I can do now. When you're like me, you don't get to do many things. *(Beat.)* Claudia was always afraid you'd come in the night and take her little sister away from her. I was once afraid of you, but you don't wear a mask like in the movies or wear that big cloak. You don't look so grim in person. *(Beat.)* Though you're not really a person, huh? *(Thinks, then graciously.)* Maybe I'll let you out some day. After I've gone on *Jeopardy* and after I've finished studying all the cards. I get tired now. But I don't tell Claudia. Claudia doesn't like to think about that. She likes to keep me in this house so I won't go away and do bad things. Claudia likes boxes. But I think there will be a time when I won't want to know things. And then I'll let you out. *(Beat.)* But wait till after *Jeopardy*. Claudia says I could be on *Jeopardy* some day.

Ismene
By David Eliet

Ismene: age twenty, youngest daughter of King Oedipus and Queen Jocasta. She is a beautiful young woman.

Dramatic

> *One year after the deaths of her sister Antigone, her brothers Eteocles and Polynices and Creon's wife and son, Eurydice and Haemon. Ismene has been trying to convince Creon to let her leave the palace and to rejoin society now that the year of mourning is over. Creon has refused her entreaties. He tells her she must remain locked up in the palace for the rest of her life to atone for the sins of her family. Desperate to know love, Ismene begs to at least be given a woman as her lover.*

ISMENE: They say the girls of Sparta learn to fight, just like the boys, that they all walk around naked until the day they are married, and that they all have an older woman as their first lover. I want a woman, Creon. I want to walk naked through the streets of Thebes, my hand being held by an older woman who is taking me home to teach me the secrets of love. Her hair is gray, and her breasts have grown saggy. My tight, young warrior's body excites her, and she is grateful that I have been given to her. And I am grateful. I am grateful that I have been given to such a good and gentle woman. And when we first get to her house, she will heat the water and fill the bath. She'll scrub my back, and rinse my hair, and then she'll slip off her robe, standing there naked by the tub, exposing to me her puckered thighs, and stretch-marked belly. And I will see myself in ten or twenty years, when my skin has lost its strength, after my firm young belly has been stretched time and time again carrying my husband's children. And when she lowers herself into the bath, I'll reach out and wrap my arms around her. And I will know love. I will know all there is to ever know about love. I want a woman Creon. I want a woman to make love to me.

Lavinia Speaks
By Jennie Redling

Lavinia Lewis: woman, twenties, African-American, hiding behind smiles and a fragile self-control

Seriocomic

> *Lavinia Lewis is a struggling actress who, among several part-time jobs, teaches children television-commercial technique. Meanwhile, her father is ill and watching his lack of desire to recover, Lavinia sees her own lifelong inability to fight for herself. Her buried anger begins to explode in silent mental tirades and verbal eruptions at the most unexpected and inopportune moments. Here, she comes into the classroom after just losing an audition because she wasn't "Black" enough.*

LAVINIA: Ubiquitous? Tell us what you had for breakfast this morning — was it real food? Ubiquitous? I'm talking to you. *(Pause. She seems bewildered.)*

I'm sorry, Jennifer. I forgot your name for a second. I'm sorry — don't cry, Jennifer, please? I apologize. Of course I know your name, honey, there's nothing wrong with your name, nothing at all.

Yes, there is something wrong with your name. It no longer represents anything — it's become a faux name spawned by some 1970s movie about a dying college girl that persuaded your mother you might evoke the glamour and distinction she lacked — a notion shared by umpteen million other American mothers — so there is now such an epidemic of your name that you and countless others are, ironically, straddled with a designation that signifies the essence of unoriginality. Your name doesn't do its job. Its job is to set you apart. Your parents must have families — a host of souls with names to call upon or if not at least a modicum of imagination — surely it's not asking so much.

The Cock of the Walk
By Melissa Gawlowski

Kristy: a woman in her late twenties

Comic

Best friends Kristy and Becca are discussing their very different opinions on men. After Becca talks warmly of her boyfriend, Kristy speaks of a less pleasant encounter and tries to set her friend straight about gender relations.

KRISTY: And then — God. Then he was all, "C'mon, flash those hog taters over here!" Men revel in finding new names for sexual anatomy. I think it's a hobby. But I kept walking. Well, I glared a little. — What, do you never read those E-mails? Women get assaulted getting groceries, I'm not confronting him and playing Russian rape roulette. Men are pigs. That's all there is to it. They eat, sleep, and think of new places to stick their dicks. Look, I know you choose to be shackled by the patriarchy, and that's fine.

    I just prefer to avoid any potential penile oppression. And I know what you're thinking. You think you can hang around a man a while and start to understand him, what goes through his mind. But you can't — it's impossible — because you don't have that certain little appendage yourself. We are the subjugated. We can only imagine what it's like to hold the power. You can think you know your cocksure friend, but in the end, Becca, he's packin' a loaded gun. And to him, we're just an empty holster.

Dreaming of a White House
By Leanna Hieber

Erin: female, twenties

Comic

> *Erin attempts to get on a plane to visit her new lover. Her ex-boyfriend Dave has tracked her to the airport to propose marriage, his reasoning being that he wants to run for president and needs her on board.*

ERIN: You need me like you need . . . another hole in your head. You must already have one because it's quite clear precious brain cells are leaking out by the thousands. Dave. I want to be a singer. I want to wail about all those red flags in that big white mansion. But I don't want to be inside it. And I WANT those crazy, kinky forays. And I want them to be INdiscreet! Thus, "Political housewife" does not enter the equation. Being the hand on your back; supportive from the shadows; the smiling wife waving princess waves in presidential motorcades — NONE of that appeals to me.

I want to live a protest-song-rock-star kind of life unchecked by popularity polls. And you say "what better way to live than by confronting that which makes you want to puke?" That statement was half intelligent, half Keanu Reeves. That's your problem, Dave. Half the time you're on the ball, half the time you're a boy who can't act.

And now you want me to keep you in line? Well I've tried for years, you don't listen. You think I want to make a career out of it? And that's just the tip of the iceberg. *(Beat, then with sudden fury.)* And why the hell is it always the woman's job to tell the man when he's being an asshole?! Figure out for yourself what makes you a dick! Why is that my job?!!

Paralyzed July
By Kevin M. Lottes

July Moore: a woman in her late twenties

Dramatic

> *July is in love with a soldier who has returned home in a wheelchair. A bombed wall collapsed on his back, damaging his spinal cord, paralyzing him from the waist down. Before he left to go to war, July promised him she would wait for his return. After considering the effects of his condition on the rest of her life, she is torn about whether to leave him or love him.*

JULY: I have tried to make this work with you like this, but I have to be honest with you, the legs you lost from that wall collapsing on you is the wall that's standing between us right here and now. There are things I have to have in order to . . . Carl, I want to dance on a Friday or Saturday night; I want to make love to someone I can wrap my legs around if I so feel like it — *and you better believe I feel like it.* I feel it all the time, but I can't do anything with it. It just clams up into a single hug, and well, hugs are great and all, a little peck on the cheek — but you need the whole body, mind, and soul to get something like that satisfied and that's what this all boils down to, Carl — *I can't get satisfied. I'm* all pent up. If you were to open up *my* insides right now you'd think *I* was the one nailed to a chair for the rest of my life! And that's just the thing — I'm not! I've got the rest of my life ahead of me and my God I'm not spending the rest of it nailed to a chair! As long as I can do something about it — I may sound cold and selfish, but come on! I need what I need!

Headwork
By Keith Huff

Jenny: twenties

Seriocomic

> *Jenny has had a rough life. Pregnant at sixteen, she gave her first child up for adoption. Now she's pregnant again and still in search of a rewarding career . . . and a husband. In this scene, she's doing a customer's hair and taking full advantage of her captive audience.*

JENNY: It's a lousy scam. The guy who signed me up to secretary school? He was this Greek guy with this Afro. Home perm or something. He did it himself. Got the back and sides all flat. So this Greek guy with hair the shape of a cheese wedge, he takes me to lunch to like, you know, sign me up to be this lousy secretary. But does he take me to Mickey D's? No, he takes me to this place called the Boneless Ox or the Syphilitic Parrot or something. I don't remember. They got tablecloths, napkins, mirrors, candles, the works. So I sit down thinking — (The cheesehead, he's pushing in my chair for me.) I'm thinking, nice place, maybe he's got more than secretary school on his mind. Greeks are like that. They get tanked up on that oom-pah wine they make outta pine trees. I been to Greektown a lotta times. Tanked up, they dance with anybody right there in the restaurant. Other guys, even. So I'm thinking, you know, see what the wedge-head is drinking with lunch and maybe I'll like get some indication. 'Cause I can't say I never in my lousy life entertained the thought of being a kept woman. I got interests. Ways of keeping myself busy. Not just bonbons and soaps, neither. No, like books. I like books. I'd read some books. And home decorating. I like rearranging things. And shopping. You wanna home decorate, you gotta do the shopping. Kids, too, I'm thinking. I'm good with kids. I like them, they like me, it's a mutual thing, and the Greek guy ain't drastically ugly. Not like car-wreck ugly or anything. He had Mick Jagger lips, sure, but I thought a decent haircut and a outfit not so polyester, the man had potential.

Sky Lines
By David-Matthew Barnes

Sarah: nineteen

Seriocomic

> *Angered over gossip she has heard about herself, Sarah attempts to put her two neighbors, Maggie and Venita, in their place. The year is 1965. She is standing on her fire escape.*

SARAH: I imagine Paris is lovely this time of year. Have you been there? *(Quick pause.)* What am I thinking? Of course you haven't been there. The two of you haven't been *anywhere*. In fact, neither one of you would know culture if it fell down and hit you on your empty heads. It's a shame, really, how both of you live these miserable lives. Boo hoo hoo. Blah, blah, blah. That's all I ever hear out of the two of you. Margaret, perhaps you felt that having a baby would give your husband some much-needed ambition. After all, driving a forklift for a meager living down at the docks will never make you wealthy. And Venita. Poor, sweet Venita. You married a man and allowed him to shame an entire race of people, not to mention the history of our country. It's difficult for me to imagine how you sleep at night with what you have done. I just pray that you never have children. If there is a God, he will make you barren. It is evident that it is my duty to uphold the dignity of this neighborhood by being a woman of high morals, good virtues and maintaining my sophisticated sense of style. You two little classless vultures will spend the rest of your lives rotting away on your balconies, staring at an empty sky. You don't even have the decency to decorate. Is it too much to ask either one of you to put up a flower box? Of course it is. *(To Maggie.)* You're too concerned that you might miss an episode of *As The World Turns*. *(To Venita.)* And you, you're too consumed with self-pity, wallowing in it like — like *shit*. That's right, I said a dirty word. You think you know me? Well, let me tell you something. It takes a lot of work to look like this. It isn't easy to be a perfect wife. But, at least I *try*.

Sky Lines
By David-Matthew Barnes

Maggie: nineteen

Comic

Fed up with her snobbish neighbor, Maggie confronts the woman, face-to-face. The year is 1965.

MAGGIE: Listen here, *missy*, with your overgrown sun hat and fake plants. That's right, I said *fake*. There isn't any water in that rusted watering can. You might fool everyone on the block with your high-and-mighty routine, but I see right through you, Sarah Isleton. You're not from Harmonville. You grew up on the south side of town, the wrong side of the tracks. In a house with a tin roof on it. Your father lost his job at the factory and since then your mother has had to wait on tables at a greasy spoon just to put food on the table. You clung to Jimmy like electricity because he was your ticket out of the squalid little life that you led. He was your one hope, your one shot at the big time. Even though the son of a bitch is dumber than a box of rocks, you laid down for him because he knew how to catch a football. He was your Kennedy, but you are certainly no Jackie and you never will be. No matter what you say or what you do, you'll still be that dirty little girl from that run-down shack of a house who tried to marry her way out of a life of poverty. I make no excuses for who I am or where I come from. My Simon might not be much of a man and I have to scrape and save just to get by, but at least I live an honest life, which is more than I can say for you. You prance around here like some sick version of Doris Day, all sunshine and *lovely* and *ever clever*, like you're waiting for the God-damned *Beaver* to come home! *(Inside her apartment, Maggie's baby has started to cry.)*

Window of Opportunity
By Barbara Lhota and Janet B. Milstein

Julia: early twenties, newly engaged

Dramatic

> *Julia, early twenties, recently engaged to David, has learned from her longtime good friend and roommate, Duncan, that he is in love with her. In this speech, she tries to convince him to move on with his life.*

JULIA: You know what? This is bull. You had four years to fall in love with me, Duncan. You had four years to act on it. For whatever reason, you didn't. Now, someone else is crazy about me and you're suddenly smitten? That doesn't give you even the slightest pause? *(Beat.)* I know you, Duncan. Your whole life has been about competition. Getting the best grades, sweeping the track team finals, competing with other freelancers for the best story. You know what I think? I found someone who loved me, and you got scared that you'd be alone. So suddenly, you're in love with me too, right? Listen, what I have with David is right, Dunc. I can feel it. And I won't jeopardize that for something I'm not sure of. Sometimes things happen for a reason. *(Beat.)* Come on now, pick yourself up sir, and get back on the horse. You're a braver man now than you've ever been.

The Audience
By Kathleen Warnock

Kelly Springer: early twenties, rock musician

Dramatic

> *Kelly and her friends are waiting to get into a rock show. A
> car has just driven by and they've had bottles thrown at
> them and been cursed at.*

KELLY: Yeah! Big men throwing bottles out of cars . . . so tough! I
know those guys. They dissed me in the parking lot in high
school. They yell shit at me when I walk into an open mike with
my electric guitar. Won't even let me touch an electric guitar in
the music store. "Girls play acoustic." I don't even OWN an
acoustic. When my band has a gig, nobody lets us use their drum
kit. They do it for each other. I've had guys fuck with the sound
board so we sound like shit. You ask someone to jam, he thinks
you're asking him to fuck. Last band I auditioned for, they
wanted me to wear a thong! I'm not gonna live in my parents'
house and work as a waitress the rest of my life! I'm gonna move
to New York, and find me a band. People keep telling me it's
dangerous, but I think it's more dangerous to sit at home and
curse the bitches who don't want to break a nail playing a guitar, and the boys who want a hummer instead of a musician.
Fuck THAT. I'll take New York any day.

Swap
By Barbara Lhota and Ira Brodsky

Nina: twenty-four years old

Comic

> *Nina and Kate are roommates and good friends. Recently,*
> *Kate has begun dating Nina's former boyfriend, Josh.*

NINA: Well, I admit I am a hair jealous. He has a job. He didn't have
a job at some fancy Geometric Research company when I dated
him; in fact, he had no job at all when he was dating *me*. Maybe
I'm just second-guessing my judgment. I mean, I thought Josh
was a lazy, good-for-nothing loser when I dumped him. I'm not
trying to be insulting. It's the truth. It's like when you're a kid
and you have pork chops and you hate them. You tell your mom
you refuse to eat them — ever — and then your best friend
comes along and loves them. Wouldn't you want to try the pork
chops again? Wouldn't you want them back to see? Oh Jeez, you
wouldn't, would you? *(Waves it off.)* You're such a martyr. I'm
simply saying that Josh seems a lot cuter and nicer since *you*
started dating him. I can't help it. And don't you think it was
rather selfish of him to pick my best friend? Anyway, I guess this
just means I respect you. Josh is kind of attractive and cool now
that I see him through you. *(Beat.)* Oh no, do you think he acted
like a loser to get out of dating me? *(Kate shrugs.)* Don't shrug!
The least you can do is disagree with me! He did, didn't he?
(Kate doesn't react.) Ohhhh. He was too cowardly to get out of
it in the normal way by just dumping me! So he went into an
entire act of being a huge loser so *I'd* dump *him!* And I did!

Key West
By Dan O'Brien

Brigid: twenties

Dramatic

> *Brigid has come to Key West in search of her estranged father, Niall. Late at night, in a back room of her father's dilapidated house, Niall asks Brigid if she was ever angry that he was not a part of her childhood.*

BRIGID: It was a comfort most of the time. No matter how bad things were, and they were bad most of the time, I always knew there was a reason. There had to be a reason, you know? . . . I had that fantasy that all kids have, I guess, that their parents aren't their parents — and I fixated on my father. I would fantasize, going to bed at night, that you or someone like you — *my real father* — was out there. Somewhere. And if I could just hold on and be patient enough, if I could wait and listen and look — for clues — maybe one day I'd find you . . .

Or you'd find me. . .

I thought I was crazy. I didn't have any proof — .

I used to wonder if you'd forgotten me. Because if you knew how much pain I was in — you'd come and save me. Right? — But you never came — why? Didn't you care? And if you didn't care — if my own father didn't care about his own daughter — what was I, then?

So I went looking for you — everything I did wrong, and I did a lot of things wrong, was my way of trying to find you. I thought — without thinking — if I just fucked up bad enough, you'd come and punish me. Or we'd meet in a ditch somewhere, under a bridge or in jail, and you'd be just as screwed up as I was, but it wouldn't matter because we'd be together, finally, and I could punish you . . . *(She's crying softly. After a moment.)* Did you ever love me at all?

St. Colm's Inch
By Robert Koon

Camille: twenty-eight

Dramatic

> *Camille, a Quebecoise farm wife, has come to California to pack up the estate of her deceased sister. She is speaking to her sister's ex-husband, with whom she has had a contentious relationship. She speaks with a French Canadian accent.*

CAMILLE: You told me that the things you did, you did because of Marie. This is for Marie, also, what I say.

I was supposed to have been a boy. My name, you know it is the name of a man, Camille, in French it is not a woman's name. And it would have been better if I had been. A boy. Or if I had been beautiful, like Marie. Marie, she was very beautiful. But I was me.

And Marie . . . when we were girls, I wished I could be like Marie. I speak English better than anyone in our town. It is because of Marie. She would read to me. It is a happy memory. It is my happy memory.

And then she left me. University, the first ever in our family. And at home, we worked. One fewer pair of hands, and less money to hire help. Marie would come home on holidays. I would look forward to them, to seeing her. It was . . . like being a girl again. And then one holiday she did not come home. And it was awful. Awful, because she did not come home, and awful because — I only knew that she had chosen some stranger over me, and I felt — It is childish, yes. I was seventeen and I was childish. But then she never came home, never, even after you . . . I thought she would see after all that she should come home. But she did not.

You see, I looked at you and I saw that you were brilliant, like she was, and beautiful, like she was, and, well, of course she chose you.

Fun House Mirror
By Dori Appel

Jill: late twenties, an investment broker, successful in her work and super-organized in her life

Dramatic

> *Jill is visiting her older sister, Amelia, soon after the death of their mother. Finally pushed to the breaking point by Amelia's haphazard but seemingly carefree lifestyle, coupled with her intrusive probing and demands, Jill explodes, "In my whole life, I've never had anywhere to escape to!" In this monologue, she reveals her vulnerability and confusion as she confronts Amelia about events of their childhood.*

JILL: Here we are, six years old and ten, and it's starting to get dark. A little while ago you slipped off to Mother's room and locked the door, and now I'm starting to get scared. "Amelia?" I call, but there isn't any answer. "Amelia?" I knock on the door, and listen. There isn't a sound. Did something in there get you? Is it going to come out and get me? I'm trying not to cry — if I cry, I'm afraid something awful will happen to me. So I force myself — FORCE myself — to walk away from that door. I go to the wicker chest where we keep our toys, and I take out my coloring book or paper dolls and the cardboard candy box that holds my crayons and scissors. All the time I'm saying to myself, "Don't be scared, don't be scared, don't be scared." Then I lay my things down on the table very carefully — without disturbing the salt and pepper shakers or the pad of paper that Mother uses for grocery lists — and I tell myself that if I cut all the doll clothes out exactly right, I'll be safe. I sit alone at the table for what seems like forever, cutting and cutting with my round, blunt scissors, and dressing all the flat, smiling paper dolls in their jaunty clothes. Then at last — oh, at LAST! — Mother comes home, and you appear from somewhere, and she cooks supper, and we sit down together and eat. Amelia . . . *(She breaks down.)* . . . I'm still coloring perfectly and cutting out everything just right, and it doesn't help! It doesn't make anything safe!

Jugger's Rain
By Ron Mark

Dulcy: twenty-five; lovely, ebullient, outgoing, caring, devoted; trace of a rural West Virginia accent; now caught in the throes of an emotional upheaval in her life

Dramatic

> *Dulcy is married to Jugger's older brother, Carney. She has grown distraught over the marriage that is falling apart; of how Carney has changed. As she talks to Jugger, Dulcy draws a parallel between Carney and their daddy (Amos), and what she had expected — and still desperately hopes to have — from their marriage.*

DULCY: Your daddy was a beautiful man, Jugger. Seemed everywhere he'd walk, the grass'd turn green under his feet. Flowers open up in his hands. Kids come running at him all screaming and laughing. I watched your mother come flying out of that door in that crazy dress of hers. Kicking up the mud. And your daddy, he'd be standing right there — tall and straight as a tree. All that silver hair, shining in the moonlight. He'd catch your mama in mid-air, twirl her around like it was a ballet. God, how they would kiss . . . So long I couldn't catch my breath watching . . . And laugh! . . . No reason. Poor as dirt, pain and suffering and sick kids. But the laughing. That deep down in the bones laughing. I never forgot it . . . I thought if I married Carney, loved him like your mama loved Amos, then *I'd* have that laughing and that love. Love that never goes away. Cause that kind of love can't die. It's too strong, Jugger. It finds a way to reach out and come back to us. Out of the grave, see, and come back home. The dead don't leave us. Ever. It's us, the living, who leave the dead. Your mama never left Amos. But me, I left Carney a long time ago. And that's why Carney's dead. Because I don't love him. That's why I'm dead too, Jugger. Because he don't love me. He just . . . *(Crossing to tree, in tears.)*
> I want my husband, Jugger. I want him back. Like he was. Like you and your daddy was. Please . . . Please. Help me.

Lone Star Grace
By Suzanne Bradbeer

Persephone: twenties

Seriocomic

> *Persephone runs a diner in small town Texas, but has kept it closed for the last few months. After finally opening up both the diner and her heart, she confronts her new friend Barbie Ann, who is about to leave her alone once again.*

PERSEPHONE: You begged me to open this diner today, and so I opened it against my better judgement, even though we don't have any black-eyed peas, but I opened the diner anyway because I could tell you were troubled about something and I liked you for some reason — liked you more than I've liked anybody since Daddy. And then Kenneth burst in, and I let him go ahead and stay too because I thought he might have a nervous breakdown if I didn't, and also because we happened to have what he ordered. And I thought, "I made two friends today, two nice friends" — especially you, Barbie Ann, because you really seemed to care so much about my daddy and the daisies and me — but now you're both just going to run off together and leave me alone after I opened up everything. You're just going to skip off to see some big field or crumby woods or some stupid old hill that used to be a Battleground and I'll never see you again. *(She pauses, embarrassed by her own vulnerability.)* So anyway. The coffee is on the house, good-bye.

Autumn's Child
By Tom Smith

Chloe: early twenties, a fragile and traumatized girl

Dramatic

Chloe, in her early twenties, has returned home with a live baby in her arms after still-birthing her own baby in the hospital. In the monologue below, Chloe explains to her momma how she lost her baby.

CHLOE: It was very quiet, after the final push. No one said a word. Then, suddenly, the doctor begins working real fast, flipping the baby over like it was a rag doll. "What is it? Why is it so quiet?" Finally the doctor looks at me and says "I'm sorry. There was no way for us to know." Why am I crying but my baby is not? "Why isn't my baby crying?"
  (Beat.)
  It never occurred to me that she was dead. The doctor tells me the umbilical cord was wrapped too tight around her neck for too long; the blood couldn't reach the brain. She had strangled herself inside of me . . . and she was dead.
  (Beat.)
  I saw them take her. My baby. They cleaned her up and then put her in a white cloth and then put her and the cloth in a metal tub. "Don't you throw away my baby! Don't you dare throwaway my baby. She's not dead! She just needs love. Let me hold my baby and everything will be alright!" Then I felt a needle go into my arm and when I woke up it was two hours later and they had thrown my baby away. When the therapist came to see me I didn't say a word. I kept silent, like in the hospital room after the final push.
  (Beat.)
  They threw away my baby! They didn't know she wasn't dead. They didn't know.

Autumn's Child
By Tom Smith

Chloe: early twenties, a fragile and traumatized girl

Dramatic

> *Chloe, in her early twenties, has returned home with a live*
> *baby in her arms after still-birthing her own baby in the hos-*
> *pital. In the monologue below, Chloe explains to her*
> *momma how she miraculously brought her dead baby back*
> *to life.*

CHLOE: They were horrible at the hospital, Momma! She was in a
drawer. In the morgue. The morgue, Momma! Marked "Dead at
Birth." Shhh, listen to me, Momma. Listen to the miracle. I took
my baby from the drawer, and I held her up close against my
heart. I knew she was breathing but they just couldn't tell. She
was breathing too delicately. I held her close. I kissed her forehead. Did you notice her hair? It's white blonde. Angel hair. I
kiss her forehead. I kiss her on top of her head. And I apologize
for everything she's gone through. There's a little tag on her wrist
with "Baby Girl Doe" on it. Momma, how can you be loved
without a name? I took the tag off her wrist, and I look down
and, still cradling her, I say, "I name you Angela." It means
angel. And suddenly she moves a bit. "Angela," I say real soft,
"It's your momma. You can breathe now. No one will ever take
you away from me again. You can live because I love you!" And
then — oh Momma! — Angela started to cry. It was music.
Beautiful music! She cried for the first time! She cried so loud
and so strong that I had to take her out of the hospital. If they
had heard her they would have taken her away from me again.
They just don't want to believe what love can do! It gave life to
Angela. Love is better than anything doctors can do and that's
why she's alive now!

Training My Hands for War
By Matt Di Cintio

Sunny: mid-twenties, petite but somehow powerful

Dramatic

> *Sunny is an unsuccessful prostitute with dreams of dancing. Over recent months and despite his cruelty, she has taken Luke as a lover. In the first act, Luke snidely offers to marry her if she can break the will of a devout neighbor. Sunny has succeeded in the previous scene, but Luke walks out. Here she catches herself in his mirror.*

SUNNY: What are you looking at? I've seen that expression a million times before, I know exactly what it means. All my life I've been trying to get that look on my face. Maybe I can't because I have too much heart. Maybe because I don't have any. My only real lover, the one with dark eyes, painted that look on his face when he left me, only his eyebrows were raised a little more. As if it were a surprise to him that he was saying good-bye. It's still a surprise to me. It's that exact look my father wore when I told him what I needed to be: on my own, free, unbound, those things, yes. That I needed to dance, spend the rest of my life moving. I have a vision in my mind of myself and whenever I picture myself I'm running. I'm running home, I'm running away from home, I'm running to the edge of the stage for my bow and my applause. And the look I have on my face is the look of someone who's gotten to where they're going. Do you know that look? I sat across from my father with my feet in perfect fourth position — in my mind they were in the air in an arch I could have taught classes about. At the table his eyebrows arched in confusion. He was, *bemused*. The poor man who tried so desperately to understand anything all his life, through wide eyes and a quarter smile. Do you know that look? No smile big enough to cause dimples, nothing big enough to leave that kind of mark. But the eyes open big and the forehead crinkles, that look. The one that looks like you're trying and you know you're trying. That's the look you're giving me now.

Throwing Stones in Glass Houses
By Kevin Schwendeman

Sylvia: twenty-eight, insecure, finds hope in the little things of life, a
      caged bird

Dramatic

> *Sylvia finds herself attending a support group at her local*
> *church. Pregnant and in an abusive relationship she faces*
> *issues of self-esteem and denial that hinder her ability to*
> *make strong decisions. Attending the support group, Sylvia*
> *recalls the incident that forced her to seek out help. We see*
> *the hardships of her life melt into wistfulness as she takes us*
> *back to the life she remembers, only to be brought crashing*
> *back into reality.*

SYLVIA: I just forgot to get the morning paper. My morning routine
wasn't any different. I made breakfast and did the dishes. I was
careful not to break any. Then I washed the clothes just like any
other Thursday. I went to the store with the thirty dollars I
always use to buy groceries. I buy the same thing every week. I
always have just enough change to buy the newspaper . . . oh
God . . . I . . . thought it would be OK . . . thought I'd still have
enough. I didn't even realize. I bought a pack of gum. I couldn't
help myself. I was the best bubble blower on the block when I
was little. If you gave me a stick of gum I could blow bubbles
around anyone. Big bubbles, double bubbles, the bubble inside
the bubble. I could do them all. Kids would come to watch me
from all over the neighborhood. I always invented new ways to
make bubbles for them. I just wanted to remember. Wanted to
see if I could still do it. So, I bought the gum. And I guess it cost
too much because I didn't have enough money left for the newspaper. I figured he could just watch the news on TV. I just forgot about the newspaper.
      (Pause.)
      He didn't have to hit me.

Heaven and Home
By Matthew A. Everett

Gabby: female, late twenties/early thirties, bartender

Seriocomic

> *Gabby is speaking to her good friend Cian. Cian is also the younger brother of Vince, Gabby's long-term boyfriend. Both of them are retreating from the troubles of their respective romantic relationships and hiding out in their friendship with one another, renting a marathon of movies to watch together, as is their custom. Gabby has finally realized it isn't doing either of them any good and rather than allow another movie marathon to begin, she stops Cian before he can pick up the remote.*

GABBY: I can't do this. This. What we're doing. You. Me. Movies in the dark on my bed. This. I can't. Or I shouldn't. I won't.

You and your brother. Together, you'd make a great catch. As it is — I've got to stop torturing myself and you've got to help me.

You take advantage. You do. I'm not saying it's calculated. You know I like you too much and I can't say no, so it's easier, it's comfortable. But you have a perfectly decent, caring, adorable guy who, as far as I can see, has reshaped his entire life just so he'd have a shot at being with you. And you're using me to avoid him. And I'm letting you. I should leave well enough alone. God knows I've got my hands full with your brother, as usual. We're always having trouble. He's the emotional equivalent of a long distance phone call. But I don't say anything because I'm normally too worried about when you're going to decide to get on with your life — And sure, you let me do all this, but it's me that did all the work so I can hardly blame you for the corner I've painted myself into.

I have to stop. Don't get me wrong. I still care about you. But I have to stop.

Temporary Heroes
By David-Matthew Barnes

Shelby: early twenties

Dramatic

> *Shelby is a waitress who dreams of becoming a pop star.*
> *Here she tells Sal, her best friend and co-worker, why they*
> *should leave together and start a new life.*

SHELBY: I'm saying, let's leave. Let's just go. We can catch a train and
get out of here. Out of Vinnie's and this neighborhood and New
York and this . . . *trap* that we're getting stuck in. Don't you
want your freedom? Don't you want to go and write and see
things and do things and just live? I wanna sing, Sal. I wanna
sing more than anything in this whole world. But I wanna be
with you. I want to feel right. We can go and leave this place and
finally get to be young. Tonight. I got your stuff right here and I
saved up my tips. There's so much more, Sal. There's so much we
haven't seen or done. We've been so busy taking care of everybody else. You know I've spent my entire life looking after my
mother. And you and your family and your brothers and sisters.
Well, what about *us?* Don't we get a chance? *(She begins to cry,*
but softly.) I love you, Sal. And I have from the first day we met.
And it's just not your eyes or your smile or the way you say my
name . . . it's your words and your talent and it's who you are
and what we've become together. I want to spend the rest of my
life with you.

A Question of Water
By Steven Schutzman

Dottie: a twenty-year-old rock singer, works as a waitress and
dreams of stardom. She loves to shock people with her behavior,
but underneath her tough persona, she's a romantic innocent,
bruised by life, taking things hard.

Seriocomic

> *Dottie has just quit her job and come home to find her
> father Tobias, Lincoln, and his younger brother Randall in
> the kitchen. The moment she enters she kisses Randall long
> and hard, in order to shock Tobias and Lincoln, and to
> rekindle her connection with Randall. Then, total strangers
> crossing paths in an early morning mist, Dottie kissed Ran-
> dall the first time. The kiss, the presence of Tobias, and the
> freedom of quitting her job ignite Dottie to improvise her
> vision of fated romance and stardom.*

DOTTIE: We'll separate, live a thousand miles apart. Our mouths will
ache until we can't stand it then we'll find each other by chance
at a truck stop in Ohio and kiss with raw hunger; bloody, achin'
kisses under the buzzin' highway lights. I'll know his mouth by
how it aches against my mouth's achin'. I won't let him touch my
body. I know Randall's too shy to do it on his own, that it'll be
up to me to put his hands in the right places. For a year, I'll deny
him and myself. Our kisses will become more and more exquis-
ite, more and more excruciatin'. My body will fill with music
and light and genius. I'll write ten songs a day. He'll see me live
on MTV, find the studio and break in while I'm singin'. When
we finally make love we won't know the difference between
pleasure and pain and we will devour each other alive. They'll
get it on tape and it will be the greatest rock video ever made.

Brian and Shevat
By Gabrielle Reisman

Shevat: early to mid-twenties, a romantic eccentric

Seriocomic

> *Shevat, pulled by a love at first sight, has fallen through the mirror suspended above Brian's bed. The two agree to live together but things grow difficult when Shevat's sister sends her telegrams asking her to come home. Here, Shevat explains a bit about the way Brian makes her feel to Silva, the couple's landlord.*

SHEVAT: Sometimes I smell the side of the bed where Brian sleeps. It smells like him.

[SILVA: *I smell Sammie's armchair on occasion. When I'm feeling lonely. It still smells like him. Fifteen years and it hasn't lost the scent. It's miraculous I think.*]

I lie on his side of the bed and delve into the smell. I smell and smell and melt into the mattress. Melt right through it.

[SILVA: *I used to fall asleep in that chair, for years after he left I'd curl up and fall asleep in it, God keep him.*]

I can feel my skin again. I haven't felt my skin since I was five or so. Out in the sun, y'know. With the sun and the breeze and the grass I could really feel my skin. And then it was gone. I forgot I had skin or that skin could feel. — But yesterday I woke up and it was there. It was all tingly and shimmerific. Like light was breaking through all my hair follicles. I could feel it growing. And dying. And laughing. Skin moves, it's always moving and dancing, and laughing all over you.

[SILVA: *I have felt my skin before, but it's rare.*]

I wanted to lie in bed and luxuriate all around in it. But I wanted to go outside and dance around in the sun and streetlights and water. It's so much. I don't know where to put it all. It's not like drugs, you don't feel burdenified. It's clean, shimmering. Like I'm breaking open into light.

Thoughts and Remembrance
By Jennifer Miller

Bernice (Bern): twenty, "radical" college student, plain, stocky

Dramatic

> *Bern enters slightly drunk. She has been going out with Josh,*
> *a Jewish actor. Bern is thrilled to finally have her first*
> *boyfriend at the ripe old age of twenty. Diane, Bern's perfect*
> *older sister, is on the couch sleeping. Diane has unex-*
> *pectedly returned home following the collapse of her flaw-*
> *less marriage. She is temporarily living on the couch, refus-*
> *ing to share her old room with Bern. A FedEx envelope is on*
> *the floor near Diane (containing divorce papers). Bern bangs*
> *into the table.*

BERN: Shit! *(She starts to laugh.)* Oh my God, he loves me! OK, I
know I'm acting stupid. Diane wake up. I have something to tell
you. It's unbelievable! I know I always told you I didn't care
about love, only about truth and justice, well, I was full of shit.
I mean I do care about that, but the way Josh listens and believes
in me and touches me. Oh my God, the way he kisses me—
Diane, wake up. Don't you want to hear about it? I'm in love.
Was it like that with you and Steven? Did you act stupid and gig-
gle all the time? Did your heart race when he looked at you?
Were you all tingly when he touched you? I don't think I've ever
really been in love before. I mean, ya know outside the family.
It's amazing — Diane wake up! Diane. Diane!
(She picks up the empty prescription bottle.)
MOM!

The Six Basic Rules
By Mara Lathrop

Louise Pettigrew: twenties, a brand-new bride

Comic

After meeting in a car crash and a wild, one-week courtship, James and Louise get married. In this scene, Louise is explaining to James why she doesn't want to go into the honeymoon suite.

LOUISE: You bashed in my fender and completely swept me off my feet. For this whole glorious week, why, I've barely even breathed since then, from that first moment of . . . impact. My entire brain has been consumed with you, James darling, cataloging you, what you say, what you do, all your parts, your eyes, your hands, the dear little hairs on your neck, your voice, your smile, your shoulders . . . Ahhhh . . . And then yesterday was the first time I talked to my mother in over a week. When I called her and said, "Ma, I met a fella, and we're getting married — tomorrow!" But was she happy for me? Was she thrilled? My mother? No, because according to my mother, I'm making a miserable mistake. Well, naturally, I defended us, James. Because my mother is NOT going to tell me whom I should love or when. And then today and the ceremony and our vows, then the cake and champagne and the rice in my hair and the limo and then the hotel and the elevator . . . And then, then I got to thinking, finally got to, you know, thinking, James. This is a very big step — he could turn out to be a con man or an ax murderer. *(Off his look.)* Well, I'm sorry, but you could, and once we cross that threshold, once we're on the other side of that door, it'll be too late. We will be married. And I mean, yes, we already are married, I know that, but in there — we'll be MARRIED.

A Rustle of Wings
By Linda Eisenstein

Mara: twenties to thirties, shy in matters of romance

Dramatic

Mara has had an unusual encounter in a bar. She has met Jewell, a woman who appears to have wings. She tries to explain to her friends Frankie and Shraine how profoundly Jewell has affected her.

MARA: My heart is fluttering, racing, faster than I can count. Like a bird. And I think, oh, I get it, that's why birds have such short life spans. That's the price of flight. Their heart outruns their life, outruns their good sense. You can't live with that kind of heart-pounding excitement, and last. I can't feel anything except this pounding, this shuddering, in my head and my chest and my knees and . . . *(She stops.)* Except suddenly, I could. There was this itching, this intense feeling crawling up my spine. And I could hear the beating of thousands of pairs of wings, like a humming. It started to fill the back of my throat with something sweet, something I'd never tasted. It got me so dizzy, I had to hold onto the table, or I knew I'd topple over. I was afraid to let go, and afraid to look at her. So, I ducked my head, and looked at the ashtray for a really really long time, until my head stopped spinning. And when I looked up again? She was gone.

Jugger's Rain
By Ron Mark

Dulcy: twenty-five; lovely, ebullient, outgoing, caring, devoted; trace of a rural West Virginia accent; now caught in the throes of an emotional upheaval in her life

Seriocomic

Dulcy is married to Carney, Jugger's older brother. Covering her fear, despair, and anger that her marriage is falling apart, she talks to Jugger about how wonderful Carney had been: the early times of romance, elation, hilarity, and his dynamic ability as a preacher. But her anguish breaks through as she reveals where Carney now considers her in his emotional life.

DULCY: Carney had your hands, Jugger. He did. Strong and hard. Rough like the bark of that tree. I loved his hands. Dirt and grease under his nails. Tobacco on his teeth. Beer on his breath. He wasn't at all like the rich boys I knew. Carney was all muscle and sweat, dreams and heart. And Kiss. God, how he could kiss me. Kiss me with his soul. Make the earth move, you know . . . and talk. All night sometimes, about the world, his dreams . . . stand right up there on that porch. Preach the devil out of them poor people that came around to hear him. All them poor sinners. Carney could scare anything out of anybody. Bring them back to the Lord. Remember old Billy Clapper? Billy the Bottle? Carney scared that bottle out of Billy for a whole year. And Mog Blue. Had poor Moggy on her knees. Screaming out the name of every man she ever did it with. Half the county. Remember the candles? How Carney'd light up all those candles in a circle? Dragged poor Moggy into that . . . *Ring of fire.* Made all those people sing and cry. Saving all those crooked, busted up people . . . He loved those people. They loved him. Come a hundred miles to hear Carney scare the devil out of them. God, that man had such love inside him. Got it from your daddy.

(Tears begin.)

All the loving in this house. All the kissing you'd do. The laughing and crying . . . And now, I'm not his wife. I'm not *anything* to him!

Lavinia Speaks
By Jennie Redling

Lavinia Lewis: twenties, African-American, hiding behind smiles and a fragile self-control

Seriocomic

> *Lavinia Lewis is a struggling actress. Among several part-time jobs, she works for an attorney. Meanwhile, her father is ill and Lavinia is convinced he might live, but he seems to be giving up. Watching him, Lavinia sees her own lifelong inability to fight for herself, and her buried anger surfaces. Here, she reaches the end of her patience with the attorney's disregard for her feelings.*

LAVINIA: But, Mr. Collins, with all due respect, it's New Year's Eve, the court buildings are closed, so this won't be filed anyway. Yes, alright, alright, I'll finish it — *(She types like a demon.)* Mr. Caca — anyone ever tell you you got a nun's fingernails? I mean there are white people an there are WHITE people and you are — I mean you are BLEACHED, Mr. Caca, you are a WAX CANDLE. No offense, but sometimes I have a hard time going to movies cause sooner or later I know I'm gonna watch white people make love and I got to tell you, that is one of the most singularly NASTY sights, like watching two folks in some fake silent ecstasy while we get to admire the results of their personal trainers. Don't once see nobody happy or smiling or caring about nobody, just two bodies starved and weight-lifted into inorganic matter, devoid of character, fixated on this worrisome, hungry, graspy, greedy dance.

Mr. Collins, it's on the file cabinet, you just gotta sign it and get it notarized and stick it up your backside. That's right, sir, you heard me right — you have your ass a happy new year.

Heaven in Your Pocket
By Mark Houston, Francis J. Cullinan,
and Dianne M. Sposito

Kay Lee Davis: twenty-two, sweet yet feisty, with her heart full of musical dreams

Dramatic

> *Kay Lee, an aspiring songwriter and songstress, longs to go to Nashville but must confront her over-bearing, domineering mother, and the career she didn't have, before she can break away. Finally, realizing that her mother has deceived her into signing over her rightfully inherited property, Kay Lee reaches the breaking point in the loss of her father, career, and trust, and reacts to the betrayal.*

KAY LEE: You never let me figure out anything on my own! It's always do as you say, follow the leader. How do you do it, Mama? Pushin' me forward and yankin' me back all at the same time! "Be a success but don't you dare leave me!" "Use your gifts but take me along." My head hurts from tryin' to figure out all your double messages. Worse, I got a big ol' pain in my heart. You tricked me out of what is rightfully mine. How could you? I'm your daughter! Are you too proud, Mama? You didn't even ask me! Is this about Daddy and how much you hated him? I remind you of him every day of your life, don't I? He was gone long before he was dead, Mama! You're mad at somebody who isn't even here! I forgave him, Mama, why can't you? Is this about the career you didn't have in Nashville because of him? That's it, isn't it? Well, you have no one to blame for that but yourself! Just 'cause you didn't pursue a career, Mama. Just 'cause you chose to drive around in a lipstick red paint job Ford sellin' somethin' other than your God-given talent! Get real, Mama. This is about what you did one night twenty-two years ago in Nashville and the mistake you made was me.

Robertson & Kyle
By Adam Simon

Blair: mid to late twenties

Seriocomic

> *As their mother gets ill and eventually passes away two sis-*
> *ters begin to unravel. In this monologue Blair is attempting*
> *to get something accomplished on the same day as finding*
> *out about her mother's death. A call to a utility company*
> *becomes charged quickly as tempers flare.*

BLAIR: *(On speakerphone.) (Extreme whisper for text in **bold**.)* We've paid our bills on time. So I don't know what you're talking about. There must have been a mix up in the mail or something. But surely there was no reason for you to turn the heat off. That's just inhumane, turning us into popsicles like it's some kind of sport or something . . . Excuse me? Don't speak to me that way please. I've dumped a ton of money into what you people do (or at least what you people are supposed to be doing) and what do I have to show for it? Huh? It's not like I can take my heat with me wherever I go. You ever think of that? And how much of that money is spent when nobody's home, answer me that? You can't treat me like this because you aren't qualified, the last thing I need is somebody — . . . *(Her facial expression twists to that of absolute shock, she picks up the phone.)* Excuse me, but my children are in the room and you were on **motherfucking** speakerphone you stupid **cocksucker**, so why don't you just **fuck off**. *(She hangs up the phone.)* Tommy, sweetheart, don't sit so close to the space heater . . . Because Mommy said so!

Get Real
By Kay Rhoads

Alexandra DuPou: late teens, attractive, bright, loves life, dramatic and optimistic, but can be narcissistic and rigid in her judgment

Dramatic

> *Alexandra DuPou has come home to find her mother preparing a "welcome home" dinner for her father, whom she has never seen, who is coming for dinner after being released from prison. Alexandra, who was born after her father was sent to prison, is a successful high-achieving young woman and has no interest in any contact with an ex-convict father.*

ALEXANDRA: Oh, I get it. This is that ancient film, *Guess Who's Coming to Dinner* with Katherine what's her name and the black guy. Well, you can take one plate off the table. He's a convict. My God. I don't believe this . . . Mother! And we are going to what! . . . sit down and have some kind of family thing? Well, not me. I don't know this man. I've never believed it, really. Not for one minute did I ever believe that my father was a convict. My father died in a mountain-climbing expedition. Mt. Kilimanjaro. It was in my fourth grade geography book. This little black speck on the picture of the mountain. My teacher said it was just a piece of rock jutting through the snow. It could have been him. The whole class laughed. So, what was I supposed to say, Mom? When I was ten and someone asked? Dad? Oh, he just offed someone but you know he's your basic nice guy throwing the ball around with his kids and washing the car on Saturdays. And now? What do I say now? Come over and meet Dad who, due to, oh, some circumstances, has never been home a Saturday in my life? "Sarah, meet my father. You know . . . the mountain climber? The one I said died on Mt. Kilimanjaro? It's a miracle. He's only been away studying the circumstances of the formation of rocks and how to break them." "Sarah, meet Dad. He's been captivated by, you know, circumstances, for something like my whole life and now he's home." He's not is he? Home. Like in our house. He's not *home* is he? Or going to be, I mean, when he shows up . . . ever . . . be *home.*

Optional
By Linda Eisenstein

Mary Ellen: twenties, normally accommodating

Seriocomic

> *Mary Ellen has gone with her fiancé, Jack, his sales manager, and his manager's girlfriend, on a weekend trip to a woodland resort in the woods. She is mortified to find out Jack's "surprise": It is a nudist camp. She has been alone, steaming, refusing to take off her swimming suit.*

MARY ELLEN: *(To her fiancé.)* A spa, you said. A "rustic resort." "Todd and Ginger go up there all the time, they absolutely love it." I can't believe I am even socializing with people named Todd and Ginger, thank you very much. Much less . . . A whole weekend of this! And you, you can hardly keep your eyes off the scenery. God! *(Gets up.)* I'm going . . . I don't know where I'm going. *(Sits down again.)* Did you notice that Ginger has a tattoo of a cartoon chipmunk on her right ass cheek? I shouldn't have to know that about her. This is Todd and Ginger's idea of relaxation? . . . A "clothing optional hot springs." It doesn't look freaking optional to me. I'm the only one in two square miles who doesn't have all her parts dangling out.

Optional
By Linda Eisenstein

Mary Ellen: twenties, normally accommodating

Seriocomic

> *Mary Ellen has gone with her fiancé, Jack, his sales manager, and his manager's girlfriend, on a weekend trip to a woodland resort in the woods. She is mortified to find out Jack's "surprise": It is a nudist camp. She has been alone, steaming, refusing to take off her swimming suit.*

MARY ELLEN: *(To her fiancé.)* See, that's the problem, Jack. I've been sitting here for what?, an hour and forty-five minutes, trying to figure it out. Figure out what I'm doing engaged to a guy who would drag me into the bare-ass naked Northern California woods — with his sales manager and his bimbette girlfriend — without letting me know what to expect. Because I know damn well YOU knew what was up here. Yes you did! You did, don't bother denying it, I can hear that little creak in your voice, the one you get whenever you're trying to push through a dubious sale. And I, gullible pinhead that I am, walked right into it. So I've been thinking. Maybe I've been asking for it — the way I've always been such a "good sport," you know? Such a good girl that I wouldn't say boo if somebody served me leftover rubber tires, I'd just smile, pour ketchup on them, and saw away at them politely until they were gone. How did I get to be like that? Is that the kind of woman I think I'm supposed to be?

A Summer Wasting
By Erica Rosbe

Joni: twenty-six, frumpy but idealistic

Seriocomic

> *Joni has been working at Cutco Knives until today. She is in the Cutco Sales Manager's office speaking to her boss, Rita.*

JONI: I don't believe in them. They are too sharp. Too dangerous. They cut bone, slice it right through with their three-part serrated-edge system and I don't think we should make things that sharp. At least not for our cutlery needs . . . I don't know if you saw the paper or not but I'm in it, me, right under the horoscopes, because I saved this woman from this creep. He was going to hurt her and he didn't because I rang the doorbell and I saw him and I pulled out the model 5 vegetable slicer and he stared at me and then at the knife and I said, "This cuts metal asshole" and he took off out the back door. And that was nice because I felt so powerful, hard-core, like I finally was needed, all my work at last worth something of goodness. Then the woman looked at me and said, "Jesus, that knife saved my life," and I realized it wasn't my power. It was the knife. The model 5 vegetable slicer, the *tool* in my hand. Not me. And I don't believe in that. We have middlemen between us and what we eat! Utensils. And I peddle them. I don't stand for utensils! This whole company revolves around gadgets that will make the dinner process smoother, slicker, prettier. I am sick of the cleanness of the Cutco cut. I am going to use my hands more! I am going to cook by ripping skin from potato and meat from bone and anything I cannot tear with my hands I will slice apart with my front teeth. Rita. I am not losing my sales position here at Cutco, I am re-claiming my right to dinner as it was supposed to be eaten. Cutco knives are sharp, yes, but my incisors are sharp too. I'm sorry. I quit.

Cutting Remarks
By Barbara Lhota and Ira Brodsky

Candie: twenty-six years old, a teacher

Comic

Dana and Candie are strangers who happen to strike up a conversation at a hair salon. Candie is a grumpy kindergarten teacher who is incensed when people say that kindergarten teachers have easy jobs.

CANDIE: I knew it! I knew that was coming. I saw it a mile away. That's the jab. Whenever a teacher complains about the least little thing, everyone always says, "Hey, don't complain. You get summers off." It wouldn't matter what I said. If I said, "But the administration makes me rip out staples with my fingernails and they force me to work with kindergartners without a teacher's assistant, which is required by state regulations. And the principal whips me and makes me work nights, ties me to the desk and uses my soul as a welcome mat, and forces me to sing show tunes and hit tambourines and other annoying instruments with my little people for forty-eight hours without a lunch break, without heat or flushing toilets or pencils!" People would still say, "Yeah, but you get summers off!"

Gentrification
By Linda Eisenstein

Mo (Maureen): twenties, a tough exterior covering hurt

Seriocomic

> *Mo's brother Jordan is visiting Mo and her partner Karin,*
> *staying overnight in their new fixer-upper house. After suf-*
> *fering through a loud night of boisterous neighbors, Jordan*
> *has been tweaking her about her "dangerous" urban neigh-*
> *borhood. When he's out of the room, Mo explodes to Karin.*

MO: *(To her girlfriend.)* I hate that shit. Being stereotyped and
patronized. From my little brother, it's downright intolerable. If
he's so concerned, he can take his suburban candy-ass back to
Claremont. Where never is heard a discouraging word. And the
faces are white and the despair is more genteel. No screaming in
the night for us, thank you, we'll just gulp our pills and pretend
it's all OK. At least here, when a woman gets beat on, she
screams "you motherfucker" and hits back, instead of trying to
hide it from the neighbors. I don't want him carrying horror stories back to Mom. It's tough enough already. She doesn't want
to come here herself, so she sent him. He's her fifth column. Why
can't she just come here, eat your casserole, pretend to like you,
go home, and dish you behind your back like she would if you
were her son-in-law? *(Sigh.)* Damn it. The weekend was going so
well, too . . .

Something Simple, Plain-spoken
By Caridad Svich

Val: woman in her twenties, angry

Dramatic

> *Val is speaking to her longtime boyfriend Hayden. They*
> *have been road-tripping for several weeks with Hayden's*
> *younger brother, Theo, in search of a lost family inheritance.*
> *As the extremely co-dependent nature of the relationship*
> *between the two, once-estranged brothers, is increasingly*
> *revealed, Val begins to feel more and more left out, and used*
> *by Hayden. This moment finds her at her breaking point.*

VAL: I'm heading back. I want to go to Prague. Travel through
Europe, visit a damn castle. I don't want to meet your dad. Or
anyone else in your family. I've met Theo. That's enough. I don't
need dog poop on my shoes and days of drinking soda pop and
pretending I'm having a good time taking a leak by the side of
the road and listening to you bitch and moan and go crazy. This
is not my inheritance. We're not fucking joined at the hip. You
want to chase a mirage of a house and some phantom money?
Go ahead. I'm not a part of you anymore. See? You were inside
me a long time and I thought "yeah, maybe, this is all I get, this
is as good as I get, so let me stick around, and put up with it;
maybe he'll come round and I don't know, we could be something together." I'm not that smart, you see? I act like I am but
I'm just a dumb girl from Georgia who thought this trip was
about something else besides your cracked family and stupid-ass
dreams. I thought we were going to discover something together, something beautiful maybe, something unforeseen. But it's
clear to me now, fucking now that we're staring at a bunch of
trees and maybe there's a damn broken-down bit of house
behind them, that there's nothing, nothing at all you want from
me except a short blast of intimacy every now and then, because
what you're really after is the possibility that maybe some of
your pain will be taken away by beating your little half-brother
to the chase; your little brother who can't even . . . he's a fucking

kid, you know, a sweet messed-up thing. A wanna-be. Yeah. But at least he's that. Cause if it wasn't for him . . . he gives you meaning, Hayden. And that is the solid truth, the kind of truth you are always seeking to find in the here and now and absolute. He gives you all the meaning in the world.

The Beauty of Life
By Barbara Lhota and Janet B. Milstein

Ellen: mid-twenties, an English teacher and good friend of Ms. Li

Dramatic

> *Ellen, an American teaching in China, tries to convince an NPR reporter to forget his big story about how the Chinese government is fully responsible for a rural area AIDS epidemic and do something real to help the people. Ellen, in this speech, tries to persuade the reporter to agree to adopt her friend's youngest child. Her friend, a poor Asian woman, has AIDS.*

ELLEN: Yeah. You and everyone you know. I know it sounds ridiculous. You think I'm crazy — we're crazy. That's the beauty of life — sometimes something that seems wholly ridiculous is the one and only thing that truly makes sense. Actually, it reminds me of the one thing I truly do love about China. The way people sometimes meet you and immediately trust you for no apparent reason. It's not based on anything logical. It's just a connection — a feeling, an intuition. *(She points to a picture on the table.)* There. That's her — Shen. She's adorable, right? *(Beat.)* Ms. Li's life has been a living hell, Mr. Diggs. She would have loved to study and go to school like us, but she was forced to work in the fields. She would have loved to travel to other places and visit, maybe write stories, but she's a woman. She would have loved to watch her babies grow up, but she donated blood to the government for forty yuan to help pay for shoes. She told me once, "When I look at my daughter, I see hope." She wanted her to go to the U.S. one day. Her hope was fading. That is until she saw you at the hospital. She knew you were the one. *(Beat.)* So are you?

The Beauty of Life
By Barbara Lhota and Janet B. Milstein

Ellen: mid-twenties, an English teacher and good friend of Ms. Li

Dramatic

> *Ellen, an American teaching in China, tries to convince an NPR reporter to forget his big story about how the Chinese government is fully responsible for a rural area AIDS epidemic and do something real to help the people. Ellen, in this speech, tries to persuade the reporter to agree to adopt her friend's youngest child. Her friend, a poor Asian woman, has AIDS.*

ELLEN: You don't force change. It just happens. I mean let's not get overly ambitious about this. Every country has had their AIDS scandal with the government handling things badly. Big yawn. You'll make people on the freeway shake their heads as they drink down their Starbucks. They'll say, "Oh, those poor people — It's shocking. It's terrible." A minute later when the traffic gets ugly — just like all things shocking and terrible in the U.S. — it will be forgotten. I know you might be naïve enough to believe if you tell this story, the government will never pull this again. But terrible atrocities have occurred constantly throughout history even when a bunch of reporters covered them. You can't change a world, but you most definitely can change a life. And I'm talking about a little girl. All these things you're saying are uncertainties. It is certain this girl will starve if she's not adopted. You're here and her mother has said you're the one. Is there anything more important than this? Really? *(Beat.)* Is there?

RiO
By Jeremy Menekseoglu

Mary: twenties, an abused housewife

Seriocomic

> *Mary is becoming more comfortable with Willy. She realizes during their first date that he is very kind and very unlike the abusive monster that she is still married to. So she is surprised when she leans in to kiss him and he shyly tells her no. She assumes that he's just nervous and tries to soothe him by telling him all about real love. She has no idea that Willy is really a schizophrenic serial killer and her life is teetering at every moment.*

MARY: Oh, I know what you're gonna say . . . I used to be the same way Willy. I was real bad at sex an' stuff. I used to like think that sex was jus' doin' it an' all. You know, hard an' quick an' done with. An' this one time —
(Stops.)
I talk a lot, I'm sorry.
(Turns away. Pause. Quickly turns back.)
But I'm jus' gonna tell you somethin' I never told no one OK? — I jus' don' want you to not get the point of my story, 'n all. OK? So — I would like jus' like — screw, an' then I got herpes from this older guy I was seein'. An' I thought my life was like totally over, you know? Wait, let me finish OK? Don' get all turned off. So anyway, I thought my life was totally over'n shit. I'd like cry myself to sleep, an' all. And then I met my husban', an' I told him of course, an' he jus' said, "Well as long as it ain't exposed I cain't get it right?" An' I said, "That's right." An' he said, "OK then . . ."
(Pause.)
Do you get it? — He wanted me anyway Willy. That was love Willy. He taught me all about love, and how to make love. That disease, Willy, taught me that sex is a gift that you give to people that you love. An' after I learned that Willy, the herpes never came back again. I know it's always there an' all, I ain't stupid, but it don' come out an' hurt nobody or myself. Love put it away. Do you get it?

The Igloo Coup
By Barbara Lhota and Ira Brodsky

Denise: eighteen to twenties, an acting major, cast as a Snowflake Helper

Comic

> *Denise, a serious actress, was extremely unhappy to get the part of a Snowflake Helper, understudy to the Snow Princess, at Northgate Mall's Christmas display. The Snow Princess role went to a grossly ill-prepared girl who flirted mercilessly with the casting director and already was buddy-buddy with the Santa Claus. Denise's jealousy turns to outrage as she realizes that the Snow Princess doesn't even appreciate the part. Denise convinces Marcie, a Candy Cane, to take part in a coup to oust the Snow Princess.*

DENISE: Jeez, Marcie, I thought we were in this together. You're gonna let this Diet Coke–drinking, heavy-smoking witch represent the Snow Princess in the upcoming Northgate Mall parade? You're going to let the sleaze suck face with Toy Soldiers in front of the innocent tots as they wave to Santa? Honey, I know you're worried. But the reason I'm so frustrated and distraught is *because* of my experience. I've been a Candy Cane. I've been the Pilgrim. I've been a Pumpkin. I know what it takes to be a good Snow Princess, and that bimbo just stole the part from me. Because she knew the big, fat red guy. Sure, if she cared about the performance, about the truth of the role, like you and I care, I wouldn't mind. I'd applaud and bow to her and give her my snowflake offerings, but she doesn't. She spits in my face! She laughs at me and even mocked me. She said I'm a flake ball. Not a *snow* ball. That wouldn't offend, but a *flake* ball. Yes! To her all I am is a flake! She told me! And even though I *am* playing a flake, I knew what she meant. Do you see how that hurts? Do you see how that destroys my confidence? When she mocks me, don't you see? She mocks all of us Snow Flakes and Candy Canes who care. Did I mention that she said all the Candy Canes sucked? She said none of you had any acting ability at all. And she makes ten dollars an hour to our seven fifty! *(Beat.)* So, you'll do it?

Tribe of Three
By Eliza Wyatt

Goli: late teens, earthy, rebellious, wears long gypsy skirts

Seriocomic

> *The play traces the fortunes of the Karimi family, refugees*
> *from Iran, who left during the Iran/Iraq war. Goli wants to*
> *use her gap year to join the Festival Circuit in pursuit of a*
> *purer more earthy lifestyle. She wears long gypsy skirts and*
> *extended hair, she has a rebellious attitude and may never go*
> *to college. She's talking to her parents who are behind her*
> *door waiting for her to come out.*

GOLI: I will come out but not to eat. It's not so much that I don't like
the food you cook, Mama, but I can't take all that rice. I want
to eat white bread sandwiches with ketchup. I honestly think if
you started to eat more like the rest of Boston, it would change
you. You'd stop thinking so much about the Middle East
because you wouldn't be constantly reminded of it by the smell
and taste of *gormay sabsi!* There'd be a metabolic change, a
lighter feeling, airy freedom and I think you'd both put aside
that terrible prejudice you seem to have against letting me do
what I want. You know there's an unwritten law giving me a perfect right to drive a car and hook up with some really mature
people who know how to put up a yurt and make a living from
the Festival Circuit. If it's being a nomadic gypsy as you say, it's
being a self-sufficient, self-employed one. And don't go quoting
the Koran to me either, because you never even had a copy in the
house until I decided to become an Earth-Spirit. If we were all
happy in tents, there wouldn't be a war in the Middle East.

I know it's sad for you to see me go. It's sad for me too. But
it's my destiny. And that's Islamic. I need green fields and fresh
air and great renewable energy sources from ordinary things like
compost. Sorry you can't come with me, but it's only a tempo-
rary separation. By the end of the summer I'll be home again and
I won't be changed that much. Not at all likely! I'll still be your
only daughter, won't I?

(Goli slowly opens door to her parents.)

Sacrifices
By Barbara Lhota and Janet B. Milstein

Stacey: young adult, Jay's sister

Dramatic

> *Stacey, Jay's sister, tries to convince her brother to allow their father to apologize to him for years of abuse. Jay is currently incarcerated for a gang-related shooting.*

STACEY: Jay, don't be stubborn! Listen to me this time! This will eat at you for the rest of your life. This is a chance to put it to rest. You don't have to see him after today. Just hear him out. You don't even have to accept his apology. But he'll validate everything you've said and more. He did with me. And his words will put things to rest! Look, you trust me, don't you? I've never steered you wrong. It's worth a shot. Right? There's no point in hating and wanting to kill him anymore, Jay, he's dying. He's gone. He only has a month or two. So I don't know if there'll be another time. I beg you, Jay, be stubborn with anything else, but this once, listen to me! Do this for you, not Dad. Do this so you can hear how right you've been all along. So you can hear him say, yes — that's the truth of what happened to you. He wants to admit it was his fault — everything, so you'll know you're not a horrible person. Then maybe you won't hate yourself so much. And you'll find some hope again. You don't have to forgive him. You can just listen if you want. *(Beat.)* What do you say?

Picture Show Video
By Kevin M. Lottes

Ami Fleets: a young woman in her early twenties

Dramatic

> *Ami Fleets has just returned home from a trip to Greece. While there, Ami experienced live theater for the first time. Her boyfriend, Johnny, works for her dad in the video rental business in a small Midwestern town. They've always watched movies on their nights together. On this particular night, Ami just noticed an ad in the local newspaper announcing that a traveling theater troupe is passing through town. Ami tries to convince Johnny to go.*

AMI: Oh, just look, Johnny! It starts at eight o'clock tonight! Can we go and do this instead of watchin' another movie? Please! I'm so sick of watchin' movie after movie; it just seems so trivial to me, now that I've experienced *live* theater. It's where you can feel the body heat from the actors rise when they hit that all-important moment, where you can feel their breath on your face, where you can hear the most beautiful words ever spoken, where people get down and dirty and *talk* to one another and where your heart battles with your head and it excites itself in a way no movie could possibly do, where you can see yourself up there, being exposed, so naked and free, and it's a one-shot deal. There's no pausing it to heat up your popcorn or going to take a piss, no fast-forwarding it, or rewinding it, it's just *there,* for you and for me, to see in passing, like some parade going by and you're a little kid again, watching it go down the street wishin' you were up there on one of them floats throwin' Tootsie Rolls at the spectators. It's a one-shot deal and I want to be there for it again. That's all, Johnny. I'm tired of the same old thing; I want something different for a change, ya know?

Marvel
By Joshua Scher

Gabriella: twenty-two, an African-American New York cop still low on the totem pole, but high in idealism

Seriocomic

> *A guy dressed as Spider-Man has climbed up a crane on the Brooklyn Bridge and is sitting on a platform hanging from it. Gabriella has been assigned to watch him nights. After an entire night of the silent treatment, she has finally gotten him talking on the second night, but she is still struggling to get a name out of him.*

GABRIELLA: Come on, man, you not gonna tell me your name? After all we bonded over and shit? A'ight. Not even like a nickname or sumptin'?
(No response.)

OK. Fine, we don't have to talk about it. I'll juss come up wit sumptin' ta call ya. Well, now, you didn't like wacko, so how 'bout Mr. Crazy-Man-Hangin-off-a-Crane-on-the-Brooklyn-Bridge? No, too formal, right? Playin', playin'.
(Beat.)

I'm not callin' you Spidey or wall-crawler, thas juss ridiculous. Yes suh. Ah. I got it. Porker. I'll call you Porker. Get it? It's the name of Spidey's secret identity. Peter Porker. Yes suh, Porker. That's it. Porker.
(Beat.)

Porker it is. Porker, Porker, Porker.
(Beat.)

Shit, I am still cravin' me some Chinese food sumptin' fierce. Some Moo-shoo Pork or sumptin'. Boneless spareribs. Now how you figure they do that? Ribs without bones. S'not natural. Think they'd deliver out here?

A Wing and a Prayer
By Ira Brodsky and Barbara Lhota

Kathy: nineteen, a college student

Dramatic

The United States is fighting a war in a Third-World country, and reports have come in about abuse of enemy prisoners. Kathy's brother, Eric, is away fighting, and she has come to suspect that he may have been involved in these misdeeds. Kathy's mom refuses to believe such a possibility, and Kathy tries to explain how it might have happened.

KATHY: I know. But it's what I think. It's how I understand Eric. I believe he wants to do good! I think he is practically blindly desperate to do good. But he doesn't know what *good is!* He thinks doing good is doing what other people tell him. I mean, we all do in some ways, but Eric will do anything for praise. He wants to be on the winning side. Here's what I fear. This is my crazy, horrible thought. That if his superiors said, "Eric, we need someone to help us out here. We have a bunch of terrorists in this building, and they won't talk unless we scare the crap out of them. And even then, maybe not, because remember, they're trained to die for their cause; and that cause is to kill us." It wouldn't be hard to convince him, especially if he was told by people he respects that this is the good and right thing to do.

Better Places to Go
By David-Matthew Barnes

Candace: late twenties

Comic

> *Candace is late to her wedding. Stuck in a roadside diner,*
> *she unloads about the horrible time she has had trying to get*
> *to the ceremony. She barely takes a breath, fueled with*
> *anger.*

CANDACE: Do you *know* what kind of a day I've had? I woke up late.
My cat puked all over my shoes. My roommate decided to bring
a criminal home with her last night and the guy stole her virgin-
ity *(Pauses.)* and *my* laptop. The landlord forgot to inform me
that they were shutting off the water in my building to do some
repair work. So, I had to boil bottles of *Aquafina* and wash my
hair in the sink. A necklace my grandmother gave me fell down
the drain and is probably lying at the bottom of Lake Michigan
right now. I got locked out of my apartment, so I took the "L"
train to Maxine's house — *in my wedding dress* and my cat-puke
satin pumps. I didn't get a manicure so my hands look like I've
been clawing my way out of Attica. My hair feels like *Crisco*
because my hairdresser decided to try a *new* product on me and
I swear to you, it smells like furniture polish. We missed the
plane from Chicago and once we finally got on a plane, they
rerouted us to Topeka because of some storm but I don't see any
rain, *do you?!* My own mother is refusing to talk to me because
I wouldn't allow my slutty sister to be in my wedding. My father
has been missing for three days and we suspect he's joined a reli-
gious cult in Arkansas. My fiancé thinks I'm a fat cow, an alco-
holic, a drug addict and a chain smoker. And right now, all I
want to do is be *un-conscious!*

Less Is Less
from *Occupational Hazards*
By Mark McCarthy

Felicia: an acting student in her twenties

Comic

Felicia has suddenly become deeply suspicious about her acting teacher.

FELICIA: I don't want to hop around like a turtle.

For one thing, turtles don't hop, anyway.

And I'm not being too literal. I don't think you really know what that word even means.

OK, that was a little mean.

But I'm really tired of hopping around like turtles or bunnies or whatever. I'm sick to death of "inhabiting" kitchen appliances and imitating frying bacon. I swear to God I will kill the next person who asks me to play a mirror game. One day it's "How does a bunny feel when it's hopping? Hop! Everyone hop!" And then the next day it's "Don't chipmunks hop? Come on, everyone, hop like a chipmunk." And then it was on to marmosets, meerkats, and geckos; there was brief pause where we spent a class watching Buffy over here — Candy? Gosh, sorry. Watching Candy over here miming playing volley ball in slow motion, and then it was back to hopping like —

Hey, wait a minute.

Why is there so much hopping around in your acting classes? What is it about hopping around that will make me a better actor? I'm starting to think it's all about boobs with you. Is it? Is it? *(She grabs her boobs.)* Is this what you think it's all about? Well, it's not! *(She lets them go.)*

You want to know why I don't want to hop around like a turtle? I'll tell you why I don't want to hop around like a turtle. I don't want to hop around like a turtle, because I'm afraid that if I do hop around like a turtle, my diaphragm will flop out onto the goddamn floor.

All right?

Missed Connections
By Barbara Lhota and Ira Brodsky

Jackie: twenty-fiveish, between jobs, wears a bright T-shirt and lots
   of Indian jewelry

Comic

> *Jackie and Cynthia are strangers on an airplane. Jackie is*
> *terrified to fly and has the need to vent all of her fears to the*
> *poor woman sitting next to her. Cynthia, the poor woman*
> *sitting next to Jackie, is a frequent traveler and sales rep. She*
> *is heading home after a long day of sales meetings. Cynthia*
> *tries desperately to avoid talking to Jackie, but as the play*
> *progresses, and the flight delays increase, Cynthia becomes*
> *more and more fearful about flying and everything else*
> *known to man.*

JACKIE: No. I know. I know I'm a pain. I'm not stupid. I know I talk
   too much. I know the unwritten rules. Most people on planes
   like to be quiet and think about things. It's sort of like church.
   You're sitting there all quiet and you know you should be reading the safety manual or, in the case of church, praying or
   smelling incense, but you get distracted. I personally start thinking about little things I need to do — clean the car, alphabetize
   the spice rack, go on anti-anxiety medication. And then the ideas
   start flowing, like maybe we are delayed for a reason. Maybe the
   plane has a loose wing. Maybe there's a bomb threat. Or, maybe
   I should have taken the earlier, more expensive flight to my
   aunt's because maybe that one was the non-death flight, you
   know? Versus this one. It's later, cheaper, but all about death!!

Missed Connections
By Barbara Lhota and Ira Brodsky

Jackie: twenty-fiveish, between jobs, wears a bright T-shirt and lots
of Indian jewelry

Comic

*Jackie and Cynthia are strangers on an airplane. Jackie is
terrified to fly and has the need to vent all of her fears to the
poor woman sitting next to her. Cynthia, the poor woman
sitting next to Jackie, is a frequent traveler and sales rep. She
is heading home after a long day of sales meetings. Cynthia
tries desperately to avoid talking to Jackie, but as the play
progresses, and the flight delays increase, Cynthia becomes
more and more fearful about flying and everything else
known to man.*

JACKIE: *(Sighs. Cynthia is startled.)* I'm sorry. I sigh when I get nervous, and boy do I get nervous when I fly. I mean with terrorists,
epidemics, global warming, you know. It's terrible. Forget
spring, straight to summer. April's like February. October's like
August. And don't get me started on the polar ice caps! And
hello! The Kyoto Agreement? Why didn't we sign that? "Oh,
clean up our environment for years to come and save the world?
No, no thank you." Do we want to suffocate? Do we want to
burn up when some asteroid flies through some hole in the
ozone layer? *(She makes the sounds and gestures of an asteroid
hitting the plane and exploding, followed by the plane plum-
meting to the ground.)* Well, we can't fly if we're dead! And even
if we don't crash, what about the sheer awfulness of the experience? A bag of pretzels with like two in it. That's it. No meals.
But oooh, we're the friendly skies. And we have leg room, unfor-
tunately it's for only one leg. *(Pause.)* You know, some people
with peanut allergies can't breathe? You open the bag and
they're dead. That's why they stopped serving them. You start to
wonder, do I have an unknown peanut allergy? I haven't had
them in awhile. I only ate them on planes, and now they don't
serve them. How will I ever know unless I open a bag, but what
if I do it and *then* . . . *(Does cut the throat sign.)* You think *Elvis*
died stupid . . .

The Pyre
By Terri Campion

Vicki Kearney: early to mid-twenties, a passionate, idealistic, middle-class woman, first-year third-grade school teacher

Comic

Vicki strives to keep positive while she prepares her third grade class for an unexpected fire drill, which has interrupted her day.

VICKI: OK boys and girls. CLASS??!! All eyes up front! As you know, like our special guest of the week — Fire Person Ms. Crawford — told you yesterday, it's Fire Prevention Week. And I was just told, at the last possible minute, that in . . . *(She looks at the clock.)* three minutes we are going to have a fire drill. So, I need everyone to close your notebooks for now. We'll come back to our journal writing after lunch. But right now, we need to QUI-ETLY clear our desks. That means all erasers, pencils, tissues, cell phones — everything must disappear. Now I'm going to close my eyes and count to five and when I open them I want to see clear desks and thirty-three little angels sitting with their hands folded. *(She covers her eyes.)* One. Two. Three. No talk-ing! Four. Five. Boys and girls are your desks clear? *(She uncovers her eyes.)* Very nice. Now calmly — we will stand. *(She gestures with her hands, rising them out of their desks.)* And starting with the first row — Jason put your palm pilot inside your desk! This is a drill. There is no actual fire, but if there were, we might have all been burned to a crisp by now because some of you refuse to let go of material possessions! Now! Sin-gle file! First row, march! QUIET . . . ly! Please. Thank you. Fol-low behind Ms. Rippo's class, I'll be right there and I want to hear nothing but excellent reports on your behavior. *(Beat.)* Aren't they cute?

Changing Attire
By Robert Koon

Barbara: twenty-four

Comic

*Barbara, after a difficult breakup, is trying to get dressed
for a blind date. She is speaking to her roommate, a flight
attendant.*

BARBARA: You don't know how lucky you are. You don't have to
spend all this time thinking of what to wear. You have uniforms.
You're lucky.

But you know what's even luckier? When you guys serve
your meals, there are only two entrees. Only two! Beef or chick-
en. God, that must be so wonderful. I am so sick and tired of
people changing their order. Everybody changes their order. You
go back to the kitchen, give them the order and then as soon as
you get back out, they call you over "Oh, miss." And it's not like
you don't have other people to take care of, but then you have
to go back in the kitchen and *they're* all snooty about it, too, and
all you can say is "Hey, it's not my fault," but they look at you
like you're out there just making things up, and you're not, and
you'd think that, my God, they've got the menu right in front of
them how hard can it be to pick something and stay with it?

And another thing. This leaving the money on the table and
just walking out. What's up with that? I hate that. Throw a couple of bills down and walk out. You go over there and it's like "I
hope they left the right amount. I hope they didn't just throw
down a couple of ones, just to look like they paid. I hope I don't
have to go chasing them down the street or anything." I mean,
what would it hurt to wait one minute and hand me the money
in person? What is this, anyway, "hey baby, give me what I want
and I'll leave the money on the table?" I mean what do I look
like, a food prostitute?

The Fainting Couch
By Jill Elaine Hughes

Julia: about twenty-six, an emotionally drained urban woman who
   is suffering from depression

Seriocomic

> *Julia is an unemployed temp worker without health insur-*
> *ance who is seeking counseling for her depression at a free*
> *clinic run by the local medical school and staffed by psychi-*
> *atry residents.*

JULIA: It was January and I was feeling generally like crap, which has
   been my usual state of mind since I was at least fifteen, but it's
   kind of been in varying *levels* of crap, you know? This wasn't
   just the winter blues — this was a crap explosion. Not even a
   crap explosion — a *runny shit* explosion. I think I can say that.
   You see, for me there has always been this basic level of crapness
   sort of hanging over the top of my head — you know, not too
   heavy, but still noticeable — which has been there for so long
   that I've just gotten used to it. Like when the muffler on your car
   just starts rattling and rattling, and you keep meaning to go to
   Midas to get it fixed, but you don't, and you start getting so used
   to the rattling that it just becomes part of the normal sound of
   your car — it becomes so natural to you that it begins to reas-
   sure you that your car can just keep on running with this new
   and interesting noise underlying its normal function, and you
   forget that anything is wrong until your whole exhaust system
   suddenly falls out of your car and your entire underbody is just
   lying in the middle of the fucking Kennedy Expressway. Only
   then do you realize that the goddamn car isn't going to run anymore without that rattling rusty muffler that you had grown so
   attached to, and you just panic. I mean really panic. Like wak-
   ing up in the middle of the night gasping for breath, thinking the
   world is going to end because your sinuses are so clogged up by
   your constantly running tears. Now, I can deal with feeling like
   basic-level crap all the time. That's just the way it's always been.

But when I can't breathe at all, and I'm turning blue and using up an entire box of Kleenex every night between the hours of three and four A.M., then I think it's time to get a tune-up. So here I am.

Cutting Remarks
By Barbara Lhota and Ira Brodsky

Candie: twenty-six years old, a teacher

Comic

> *Dana and Candie are strangers who happen to strike up a conversation at a hair salon. Candie is a grumpy kindergarten teacher who wants to go off on people who want to blame students' failure on the teachers.*

CANDIE: When I first became a kindergarten teacher, I felt I had to uphold the image of the perfect teacher. I bought a laminating machine. Every good teacher has one at home. I laminated everything. If I met you, I'd probably laminate you. Anyway, my fiancé, at the time, was depressed. So I thought I should be very up to counteract his depression. I'd come home and talk about clay and Bob the Builder and how happy I was. "I'm so happy." And one day little Larry decides to put dirt up the noses of several of his little pals — "fun age," huh? Several parents call inquiring how the dirt got up there. I wanted to tell them that we were trying out some new horticultural adventures, but instead I apologize and explained about little Larry. And even though my relationship was going to hell, I smiled and bounced around the classroom, "I love you. You love me. We're a psychotic family." I came home to my fiancé that night and he had taken a bat to my laminating machine. Not exactly a bat. Well, he said he knocked it over. But believe me, it was deliberate. He told me he wanted to leave me because I had told him to look on the bright side twenty-one times. He counted. He said that I may act happy or even think I'm happy, but underneath I was boiling angry that he and all these children were zapping my energy. And instead of expressing it, like a *normal* person, I was acting happy and kindergarten-teacherly, forcing him to take on my boiling anger. I thought he was dead wrong until I told him to "Shushee up, get his coat, and line up by the door so we could run off all that bad, bad energy."

Cutting Remarks
By Barbara Lhota and Ira Brodsky

Candie: twenty-six years old, a teacher

Comic

> *Dana and Candie are strangers who happen to strike up a conversation at a hair salon. Candie is a grumpy kindergarten teacher who wants to go off on people who want to blame students' failure on the teachers.*

CANDIE: They always want to blame the teachers. *(Looking up.)* But what about the parents? It's always that *we're* incompetent. *We're* overpaid. *We* need more education. What about the parents? They don't need an education? They can be dumb as bricks. Half my students come in and they don't even know their real name, let alone how to spell it. *(Kid voice.)* "I don't know my name. My momma calls me Fifi." More than half us teachers have two degrees. I only have one, but I was a straight-A student. Well, three Bs and a D in Physics, but those were dumb classes. And that's not the point. I plan to go to grad school! Once I pay off undergrad. Twelve million years from now. "Oh, get educated on soft subjects like sympathetic behavior." What about a little sympathy toward us? We're stuck with your brats every day! *(Tosses down her magazine.)* I read articles on this "No Child Left Behind" stuff and get all worked up. Sure, it's good to focus on education, watch out for kids, but I have been doing this for a while now, and not just kindergarten, and let me tell you, there are some children we should leave behind. If we don't, they'll teach the others and take over. In fact, there's at least two, I'd like to ship off to Canada.

Bridewell
By Charles Evered

Kristen: twenty, a student, obsessed with her weight

Seriocomic

> *The play takes place in the main living room of a women's sorority house on the campus of a small liberal arts college. Kristen commiserates with her sorority sisters about men and tries to console Amanda's broken heart by explaining how she would cope with it.*

KRISTEN: Look, just be glad you're not me. If you were me you'd be on your second box of Twinkies by now. I love food at a time like this. I wish I could eat for you now. Come to think of it, I probably will later. I remember when . . . I can't say the name . . . but when "a certain someone" RIPPED MY HEART OUT. It was my total low point. I was going to those Overeaters Anonymous meetings with my mother — which is kind of ironic, because she's the person who used to shove food in my face all the time anyway. So, this "certain someone" DUMPS me and as my mother is driving us home it's like; what do ya know, she just happens to stop at a Rite Aid and out she comes with a ten-pound box of candy and all I remember after that was seeing our twenty pudgy little fingers pulling and twisting and gouging out the candies and me just shoving them into my mouth and that's when I got this great idea; "I won't eat them," I thought. I'll just chew them. If I chew them without swallowing, then I never will have eaten them at all. And all of this will have been nothing but a bad dream. So I put like fourteen of them in my mouth and I just *chomped,* but without swallowing, feeling all the chocolaty juices sliding down my throat and my brain flooding with endorphins and after about eight minutes I hacked out this huge ball of nougat and caramel and deftly wrapped it up in a napkin and calmly put it on the dashboard and repeated the process over and over until all the candy was gone. So, I'm sitting there, candy wrappers all over me and sweat pouring down my forehead and my mom turns to me and says, "Ya know what Pudgy-Poo, we can freeze those hacked up balls. No use wasting good candy."

Robertson & Kyle
By Adam Simon

Mackenzie: female, early twenties

Dramatic

> *As their mother gets ill and eventually passes away two sisters begin to unravel. In this scene Mackenzie enters a Church of Scientology looking for some answers to the recent death of her mother. An employee of the church has just asked "How can I help you?"*

MACKENZIE: *(Quietly.)* Um, hi. I'm here for uh, services . . . or a consultation. I'm not sure what terms you use for your worship . . . Sorry, for your dialogue. I just saw John Travolta on TV a little while ago, that's how I found out about the church, and he and his wife just seemed so at peace and I happen to be in a bit of a bind and figured it was a time for a change — I make it sound like I have a hangnail or something. Uh, I'm here — to be more accurate — because of my mom. See, she's dying and quick and it could have been . . . There's this doctor that she saw, that we saw, forever and she wasn't feeling well for a while (a couple years maybe) and he couldn't figure it out and she asked if she should get a second opinion and he said "They'll just tell you what I'm telling you." And so she didn't do anything. And of course it was cancer, I mean you knew that was how the story was going to go right? Well, I'm here because I can't seem to strike up an interest in going to church like I used to, and I need to know something. I need to know what the Church of Scientology would have me say to this man, this doctor. Because I know I need to tell him something, but I need to make sure it's right. So what would the church say about that?

Gray
By Tom Smith

Laura: late twenties, a take-charge advertising executive

Dramatic

> *Laura, in her late 20s, discusses her pregnancy with her longtime boyfriend, Matt. Matt has been secretly carrying on with a young street hustler, Pack.*

LAURA: *(Laughing.)* I wish I had a camera right now! I tell you that Shauna wants to throw me a baby shower and you look like you're about to throw up. *(Beat.)* If you're scared you can say so. It's OK. I am, sometimes. Actually, I am a lot. It's just that I see my friends with their kids, and they all seem so content, so at peace. But me? I'm just restless all the time. It finally occurred to me that no matter how successful my business gets, or how great my apartment looks, it's never going to be more important than having a child. I never thought I'd feel that way. Ever. And I'm terrified because I think I'm going to be a horrible mother. I'm not what you'd call warm and cuddly. I've purposely chosen to focus on my career. When this happened two years ago, I didn't give a second thought to not having it. But now . . . Oh, God, I just need this in my life right now! I don't know why, but I do. And I hate that I feel like a failure for wanting to be a mother.
(She breaks into tears.)

I can't believe I'm freaking out like this. I hope to God this is just the hormones talking. *(Beat.)*

Matt, I want you to be really honest. Even if you think it's going to hurt me. Should we have this baby? Even though we're both freaked out about it? Matt?

Gray
By Tom Smith

Laura: late twenties, a take-charge advertising executive

Dramatic

> *Matt, who considers himself heterosexual, has been strug-*
> *gling with his growing attraction to Pack, a charismatic*
> *street hustler. Wanting to end this attraction, Matt*
> *drunkenly attacks Pack and runs off. Pack has just visited*
> *Laura, Matt's pregnant longtime girlfriend in her late twen-*
> *ties, and tells her about the attack. In the monologue below,*
> *Laura confronts Matt.*

LAURA: I left you three messages on your cell. You didn't call me
back. Where were you? *(Beat.)* Matt, what's happening to you?
Is it me? Am I making you feel this way? Is it the baby? Please,
Matt, talk to me . . . Pack came by here tonight. He told me what
happened. *(Beat.)* How long have you been seeing him? How
many times have you lied to me about going to meetings or grad-
ing papers when you were really seeing Pack? Is this why we're
not married? Because . . . ? You've humiliated me. All these
years, just thinking that you were too much of a commitment-
phobe to — Who else, Matt? What other guys have you kissed?
Or screwed? You don't expect me to believe that Pack of all people . . . ? I don't know if it's a midlife crisis that's come ten years
too early, or something you've been repressing, or because you're
too scared to be a father, or — I just know I don't trust you anymore. I can't forgive you, Matt. I don't even feel safe around you
anymore. I don't want to see you for a while. Not until you've
decided what you really want. Who you really want. But you'd
better make up your mind pretty soon because I am having this
baby and I need to know whether or not it's going to have a
father.

Women in Heat
By Rich Orloff

Marge: twenties

Comic

While vacationing in Key West, Marge, a conservative woman from Ohio, advises a friend who is considering a sexual adventure.

MARGE: It's — I just, I just think we live in a time when everybody's looking in the wrong direction for happiness. If you're not happy, pierce your navel and tattoo your back. And when the happiness fades, pierce your eyebrow and tattoo your butt. And when that happiness fades, pierce your tongue and tattoo your arm. Pierce this, tattoo that; pierce this, tattoo that. And one morning you wake up and you're still not happy, but your body looks like Swiss cheese with decals. My point is, I've tried things. Lots of things.

But when Barry and I broke up, I didn't think, well, "At least I've had adventures." I thought, "I'm no closer to happiness than I've ever been." And, and then I looked at the chocolate sauce on my linens, and the scratch marks on the bedpost, and I thought about all the money we spent on rope and licorice, and, and I wondered what's the point? And then I watched the video-tapes and . . . I hate this generation. I hate the pressures, the expectations. I'm so sick of having to be part of "The Young and the Horny."

Sky Lines
By David-Matthew Barnes

Venita: twenty-one

Dramatic

In 1965, Venita, who is black, has been ostracized by her family and friends for marrying a white man, George. Here she tells her neighbor and best friend, Maggie, what she expected out of marriage.

VENITA: I imagined my life differently when I was a girl. Perhaps I'm just a fool, but I expected flowers and poetry and weekend get-aways to the country. A drive in a convertible with the wind in your hair. Something special, magic. Don't get me wrong. George and I had a very romantic courtship. He was the perfect gentleman. I felt so lucky when we met. Never in my life had someone paid so much attention to me. He's handsome and smart and he comes from a good family. *(Pause.)* Maybe it's me. Maybe I've gone crazy. It's quite possible that insanity is running in my veins. My grandmother went crazy a few years ago. One day, she started to sing. It was a song from church, one of her favorites. At first, we all thought that she was just expressing her faith for the Lord. But, she wouldn't stop singing. Even when the doctor came. She sang so much, her throat went dry and she coughed up blood. A few days later, they took her to a hospital. I've never seen her since. *(Pause.)* I'm a newlywed. I should be the happiest woman in the world. But I can't stop having these crazy thoughts. Maggie, it's almost too much to bear. I feel like a prisoner in this apartment. I sit here all day long filling up my recipe box and making shopping lists and ironing baskets of clothes. I wait with anticipation for the phone to ring because I find myself craving conversation. Anything to kill the silence. I hate the silence. It's as if someone has died and we're not allowed to speak. That's what my days are like. Deathly quiet and still. Maggie, I can't quit school. It would be the end of me. I want to finish and get my degree. I'm sure I could find work. In an office. In a museum. Even a restaurant. Anything to get out of this apartment, this coffin that I'm trapped in. It's choking me.

Southland
By Allan Staples

Abbey: late twenties to thirties

Seriocomic

Abbey is talking to her ex-boyfriend.

ABBEY: The other day I was out driving around and I went up to the Griffith Park Observatory. And as I'm looking down on the city, I had this really odd thought. I could go out to the bar, eat a Burrito and have sex with a midget and, odds are, chances are someone else out there probably had the exact same day. And I know a lot of people live here but I felt so unimportant and totally irrelevant. I felt like shit. But not the day-to-day shit feeling, but this "Big Picture" shit feeling. And I didn't know what to do. I started to freak out. I felt like jumping. But instead I sat down and made a list, you know how much I love making lists, I made a list of what has made me feel not like that. What, in life, has made me feel good. And it kills me to say this Monty, but you were the only person on my list. I realized the only time when I've felt different or the least bit special was the time when we were a couple. And maybe that's not love but I do know that I will not ignore how I feel because . . . I'm scared or whatever it is I am.

Twin Towers
By Ira Brodsky and Barbara Lhota

Janice: late twenties to thirties

Dramatic

> *Several years ago, Janice's husband died in the World Trade Center attack, and six months later, her best friend, Rose, adopted a child in Russia. Now Rose has come to New York to ask Janice if she would be the child's legal guardian in case of Rose's death. However, Janice is afraid of taking on this responsibility.*

JANICE: You asked me if I wanted to be Lola's guardian in case of your death. And a million thoughts went through my head right that second. God, I would love to be a mom. God, Lola is an adorable child. Could I do it? I think I could. Would I be OK at it? I think so. But, Ro, I want my own life too. I like going to the movies and restaurants and the gym. I like going out with my girlfriends. I may want to get married again and have kids of my own. What I'm saying is that I'm not Supermom. Sometimes I'm short-tempered. Sometimes I'm preoccupied with silly stuff. Sometimes I get really busy with my life and I'm not available to get together. Sometimes I am so blue I can barely get out of bed. I think about my husband and that plane and the pain he felt. And I will never know if he is one of the ones who jumped — *(She clears her throat to stave off tears.)* Oh boy, oh boy.

Bread and Circuses
By Jo J. Adamson

Nellie Bly: twenty-nine, petite woman with reddish hair

Dramatic

> *Nellie Bly, pioneer newspaper reporter for the* New York
> World, *gained world fame when she beat Jules Verne's fic-*
> *tional character Phileas Fogg's record for traveling around*
> *the world in eighty days. Now, nearly thirty years old and*
> *still a newspaper reporter, she's on a bus heading home after*
> *a grueling interview. She meets an older man, Robert Sea-*
> *man (a man she will marry) and explains to him why she's*
> *no longer the crusading firebrand reporter she once was.*

NELLIE BLY: I was seventeen when I dreaded the thought of being supported by well-meaning friends and relatives. In a few short
months I'll be thirty. The age when a woman becomes a joke. A
pathetic burden on society. No, the thought of being supported
is no longer odious. Perhaps I've reached a saturation point. I'm
sick to death of meeting deadlines, running after trains, sleeping
in strange hotel rooms. I'm tired of interviewing men who dis-
like me merely because I'm not of their gender. Of the women
who feel I betray them because I'm uncomfortable with a tea cup
in my hand. I'm sick of the pressures of the job; of feeling like a
machine that grinds out words to feed a stunt-hungry public.
This morning I asked myself a question that had been nagging
me for the past year. What are you doing here Nellie Bly? I had
no answer. I knew only that I didn't want to be in a railroad station in the cold dawn light. I wished for all the world to be
back in my mother's house. I wanted her to feel my head for
a fever and ask where it hurt. I wanted her to call me Pinky
once more.

Sally Sees the Light
By Barbara Lindsay

Sally: twenties, is an office worker with no great ambitions beyond finding a good husband and being in style. She's sweet and nice and maybe a little shallow. She has never been, never wanted to be, particularly deep thinking. Until now.

Comic

> *Sally and Jennifer are having lunch after a shopping expedition. Everything seems perfectly normal. They've been talking about boys, lipstick, clothes, all the girlie-girl topics they relish. But somehow, for no reason she can explain, everything has started to look just a little bit clearer to Sally. Suddenly, normal looks disturbingly askew.*

SALLY: Jeffy gave me this dress. Does that seem weird to you? I don't know, I just can't imagine buying him a shirt or a jacket or anything, especially if he's not there to try it on. A tie, maybe. Ties are safe. Ties are sort of strange, though, don't you think? This little flap of fabric hanging down a guy's shirt. You know what I mean? All knotted up around his neck and then just sort of — hanging there. I mean, if you think about it, it's really a bizarre thing. What's the purpose? How did it get started, men wearing these cloth things around their necks? It had to start somehow, but I'll bet not one man in a thousand has any idea, or even thinks to wonder about it. Do you see what I'm saying? They just knot this thing around their necks every morning and go to work, and now they're all walking around with these colored strips flapping and nobody even notices. Actually, the whole idea of clothes is just, it's just, strange. I mean, who do we think we're fooling? We're all naked underneath. Everybody's got basically the same equipment, B for boy, G for girl, but we cover it all up as if it's not there or it's bad or we don't want to know about it. Even though everybody's got them, and they're really the, the source of life even, we say they're nasty and then we cover them up and pretend not to notice. Except it's all anybody really thinks about, really. I mean, my God, all anybody really thinks about is sex! It's in songs, it's in commercials, it's in movies, it's the first thing you think of when you meet a guy, but have you ever watched it? It's nothing! It's ludicrous! It's pushing and sweating for maybe an hour at the very, very most and then it's over! It's gone! It's meaningless! What do you get? Orgasm! But what is that? You throb for ten seconds. My God, think about it!

Water Pressure
By Darren Callahan

Ashley: twenty-one, a wealthy New York socialite

Dramatic

Ashley's father died in 1939. Now, in 1959, she and her three friends slowly discover all their fathers were involved in a secret time-travel club. In the context of the play, the monologue is spoken to the audience, presumably to a boyfriend.

ASHLEY: See these? *(Ashley shows off her legs.)* Pretty trim, huh? The boys like my legs. "Ashley," they say, and whistle sometimes, "you got legs that go for miles." I tell Ginger that hers are better, but it's a lie. It's *these*. Rawwwwr. Do you want to touch them? I'm not wearing any hose. I gave that up in early '58. Pride and joy, these pipes. One day they'll get me a husband, who'll whistle and stop in his car — I like European cars — and take me for a ride down Park Avenue. And we'll neck. I'm a good kisser. Second best quality to the legs. These. Them. Film-star legs. Luxury legs, as my father might say, he who liked things luxurious. *(Pause.)*
    One night last year, I came out to my brand-new car — European — and I found a note. Want me to read it? I keep it in a drawer, but I brought it tonight for you to see.
(Shows note to audience.)
    Fifteen words.
(Counting on fingers while reading.)
    "Don't go driving. You will crash and your legs will be amputated. I know this."
(Pockets note.)
    Typed. On a typewriter. Needless to say, I didn't get in the car. Now I treat these legs like a gift from God. *(Pause)*
    They sure are nice. Aren't they?

The Age of Cynicism or Karaoke Night at The Hog
By Keith Huff

Ellen: twenties

Seriocomic

It is Ellen's lifelong goal to be married and have a family by the time she's thirty. Here, at twenty-nine, she's on a blind date with Gary and the clock's a-ticking.

ELLEN: How many men do you think I've had sex with? Not how many times. How many men? Ballpark. They say you can tell by the number of lines under the eyes. If it's a big purple and black bar under your eyes, though, it's over fifty. Nobody keeps count after fifty. Crazy people, OK. Let me see your eyes. How many have loved thee? Let me count the lines. *(Gasps.)* I don't see any lines, Gary. None at all. My God. Don never mentioned he was fixing me up with virgin territory. I feel like Columbus discovering America. Land ho! How did a prime cut of beef like you manage to stay wrapped on the freezer shelf to the ripe old age of twenty-nine? Your ears are red. They're in flames. *(Southern accent.)* And lawdy, they's a logjam at the delta, Cap'n Andy! *(Drops accent. Dead serious, intense.)* I've been around the block many, many times, Gary. Count the lines under my eyes. I'll show you the ropes. Let me initiate you. Let me welcome you to the human race.

Natural Selection
from *Crazyology*
By Frank Higgins

Lois: mid to late twenties, a career woman in advertising

Comic

Lois is having lunch with a girlfriend. The girlfriend has just asked Lois whether Lois's lifestyle of having so many men in her life is natural.

LOIS: Did you hear about that pro basketball player who claimed he'd had sex with twenty thousand women? Now if a woman had sex with twenty men and talked about it, people would say "slut."

But my life changed when I heard the truth about sperm. See, it used to be that scientists thought all human sperm behaved the same, that they all try to make it to the egg, and there's this big traffic jam and only one can get in.

But that's not the way it is. And we know this now because of these little micro cameras? Skip how you get the camera up in there — but the cameras show that only about one-third of the sperm try to reach the egg. The other two-thirds of the sperm line up and make a wall. Why?

And the theory is, these sperm, who are all from the same male, are trying to make sure one of *their* teammates makes it to the egg. And the reason they line up is that they're trying to stop some *other* male's sperm from getting to the quarterback.

We're talking natural selection. You would ovulate, and then do it with more than one male.

And to this day the sperm in this room right now still behave the same way. Which means that you and I still have it in our genetic makeup to want all the best males in the room. It's natural.

So it gets me to thinking, who *are* the best males in the room?

The Honeypot Redux
By Chance D. Muehleck

Sholey: mid-twenties, an attractive young woman who's smarter than she sometimes lets on

Dramatic

> *Sholey's first sexual encounter was with Kick; she was a child, and he an adult. She has returned to Kick's home only to find herself falling in love with him. Here, she reminds him of their first meeting.*

SHOLEY: Touch me. *(Pause.)* You know how long I thought about you? About doing things with you? I couldn't shake that feeling. I was ten years old when I saw you. I'm sure you don't remember. But I do. You were my first crush, Kick. My longest crush. All you did was smile, at first. A razor of a smile. Leaning against the back door, smoking and tilting your head. Your body in a question mark. Asking for me. I felt liquid. Transparent. Then you got close. You reached out your big hand and put it on my thigh. I liked your fingernails. They were smooth and trim. The hand slid up and the thumb licked my nipple and I said "Oh" and you said "Shhhh." Like cool wind blowing over poppies. I guess you're not supposed to covet that kinda thing. I tried to hate you for it. But you kept rising in my memory. No matter how aimless the road got, even if I quit college, I always knew there was you. That I'd see you again. *(Pause.)*
I came back to satisfy a recollection.

Women in Heat
By Rich Orloff

Kim: twenties

Comic

*One morning while on vacation with two of her girl friends,
Kim admits she had an uncharacteristic sexual adventure the
night before.*

KIM: I wasn't drunk. Or stoned. I was, I was curious. I mean, here we
are in Key West — hot, sexy Key West — and well, I was dancing with these two guys, this totally cute white guy and this
totally awesome black guy, and at one point I said, "I can't
choose between you" and the white guy said, "You don't have
to." And I laughed — and they didn't. They were *smiling*. Biiii-
ig smiles. And I thought, *this* will make a good vacation story.
And I, I don't know. Ever since I woke up, it's like there's a
debate squad in my brain. "It was a mistake" "It was fun" "It's
bad" "It's good." I mean, it's not like it was a *romantic* evening.
I didn't think, "Gee, I hope I get both of their phone numbers."
But there was something about being massaged by four hands,
being kissed by four lips, grabbing both their . . . Just once, I
wanted to go too far. All my life I've been so — Ohio. I think
Ohio. I dress Ohio. Just once I wanted an out-of-state experience. All I wanted was a taste of Key West, one taste, and then
I'd return home to a healthy diet of Ohio. But what do you do
when you discover you have taste buds you never knew about?

The Metric System
By James Armstrong

Mary Beth: a woman in her twenties

Dramatic

> *Susie, a tame suburbanite woman, has found her life entan-*
> *gled with that of Mary Beth, a waitress in the city with a*
> *rather unconventional lifestyle. In this scene, Mary Beth*
> *tries to give Susie a lesson in the ways of the world.*

MARY BETH: Sex isn't about love. If that's what you came for, forget
it. Sex isn't about caring. And it certainly isn't about sharing
yourself. It's about power. Sex is about getting what you want.
What do you want from a man? Money? A job? Someone to say
you look pretty in a new dress? Then I'll tell you how to get what
you want. Of course they'll use you. But aren't we out to use
them, too? Don't be bitter about it. Just play it out. You give
what you have to, you take what you want. Just a matter
of what you want. For some people it's dinner and a movie, for
others it's whips and chains. For others it's . . . There are . . .
ways . . . to meet people . . . After a while, the sex becomes less
important. It's the thrill. Never liked sex anyway. Never even
came until I was twenty-two . . . in the shower . . . alone. . . . But
that never stopped me from pouring hot wax on a guy's crotch.

If This Isn't Love
By Jonathan Bernstein

Cherry: twenty-seven, runs her own one-woman escort service; her
    body has the unlikely proportions of a blow-up sex doll blown
    just a bit too far

Seriocomic

> *Cherry has run into an old high-school acquaintance — as
> they engage in some sober catching up, Cherry is unapolo-
> getic about the choices she's made since graduation.*

CHERRY: Oh that's great, yeah, that's great, good for you. You *were*
    Most Likely To Succeed, 'n all that, so that's, that's come true,
    that's good, good for you. You 'n me, we done pretty good. We
    showed 'em, huh? I got a good job, too, ya know. Yeah. Yeah,
    I'm working all the time, s'been crazy, I'm really working like
    mad, s'been good, I been going good.
        What's that? Oh, I'm running my own business. Yeah uh,
    people call me. Men. Men call me. For favors, and that — that
    kinda thing — I'm not gonna lie ta you, there's no reason, I'm
    not gonna cover it up or anything, I'm proud of it, ya know, I
    help people. Way I see it, I'm like a social worker. That kinda
    thing. And it's on my own, I don't answer to no one.
        'N so what — I like what I do, ya know, I like what it is —
    ask the other girls we grew up with how they're liking *their*
    life — I got no complaints.
        'N listen, let's get this straight: I don't sell my body. All
    right? I still have my body when it's over. S'all these moralizers,
    these Christ-complex goody-gooders who're preaching they're
    gonna save me, rescue me, ya know, lift me up, talkin' salvation,
    'n I think bullshit, ya can't save me, I don't need ta be, I don't
    want ta be, I'm not waiting ta be saved. I'm not one of those
    squeaky heart-a-gold movie hookers, like in *Pretty Woman*, ya
    want Julia Roberts, ya can rent *her* at Blockbuster.
        Just live 'n let live, is what I say, 'n let me do my thing.

God Dancing
By Marki Shalloe

Ruth: twenties, African-American woman

Dramatic

> *Ruth was given to her father as a child because her mother*
> *couldn't handle her and her father didn't want to pay child*
> *support. Her father has recently thrown her out so she*
> *returns to her mother's where she desperately wants to*
> *belong. Ruth is attempting to seduce Preacher Roy,*
> *her mother's boyfriend, whom she fears will convince her*
> *mother to throw Ruth out of the house.*

RUTH: So, Preacher Roy, you like visitin' my mama's house?

I like it here, too, real well, didn't think I would but now I'm here it fits just fine.

Seein' as how you think you guide the morality of this household, Mama comin' to you 'bout all this house's business, mind if I ask you a moral question?

What if there was a gal whose Mama couldn't take her, so her daddy did?

Then she grew big and Daddy decided having a grown daughter in the house was the reason he wasn't gettin' any women.

What you think, Preacher Roy? You wanna take that girl in? Didn't think so.

This is a good house, Preacher Roy. A house of God-fearin' and pious-appearin' women, always has been, and I bet you just figurin' out I wouldn't make a good pastor's daughter 'cause I'd say "shit" in front of your parishioners.

So you gon' quit my mama 'cause you don't want my mouth ruinin' your Sunday service?

Or you gon' try to get me gone instead?

Don't bother you rubbin' Mama's titties against your Sunday suit 'til folks start sniffin'. . . then pushin' her like a tick you pickin' off — Denyin'.

Don't bother you she think you gon' be the next husband in

this house, while all the time you worryin' what folks gon' say about my pants slidin' down my crack — Denyin'. What does bother you, Preacher Roy?

Me touchin' you where you been thinkin' about me touchin' you?

Your cock's crowin'

Come on Preacher Roy, deny her the third time.

Fun City
from *Twinges from the Fringe*
By Bob Jude Ferrante

Myrna: an actress, twenties, shy, librarianish, with coquettish streak

Comic

> *Myrna came to the City with one burning ambition to be a hooker. Here, she tells the story of how she was sidetracked into acting. (Music: Cool, smoky jazz music, like, heavy sax action. Myrna comes out in a trench coat and spiked heels. She lights and drags heavily on a cigarette, blows the smoke out over the audience.)*

MYRNA: Myrna. Myrna Flotzkengruschnimmer. You know my story. Small town, Cole's Drugs. Two years. A lotta Tampax. I had a dream — to be a *hooker*. Finally I take that Greyhound to Fun City. Nest egg goes for an apartment I pound the pavement, learn the biz. The men. Not interested. "Get lost, we see hundreds a broads like youse every day." Six months, nest egg's gone. A lotta Tampax! Out on Bowery. Guy goes, "Sweetheart, buy you dinner?" I go, "Sure. I'm trying to break into prostitution." He goes, "Sweetheart! I'm a pimp! We'll discuss it" I go home, get dolled up. Thinking, "Careful girl, says he's a pimp, maybe it's a line . . . " At six I'm there: Low-back outfit, fishnet stockings, hair up. Guy — Murray Steinoblatski — gets a table. Whispers. Waiter nods. Then: Food. Wine. Should be careful — can't hold my liquor. Two bottles later, I spill it: Flat on my back 'cause I can't get flat on my back. Murray goes, "I'll start you up in pro biz." In Murray's Jag, streetlights whip by, mind's racing: "Is this it — the big break!" But we get there: Stanislavski teacher, voice coach. *Murray's an agent!* A put-up job! Out comes the hard stuff — Pinter, Miller, Shaw. Two apes pin me down and Murray forces me to . . . *act*. Bastard! *Want to rip off that smug smile*. But . . . doing *The Homecoming* " 'e finks 'e knows about 'orses." There's this sensation . . . down *there*. I got a — maybe it's sick? — MOTIVATION! Murray says, "Kid, you're a natural." I throw up. I'm turned out. *Henry IV, Part II* next Tuesday on *Great Performances*. But you know my story. Can't save a dime in Fun City.

(Blackout.)

Rights and Permission Acknowledgments

Gawlowski. Reprinted by permission of the author. All inquiries should be addressed to mgawlowski@hotmail.com

CUTTING REMARKS by Barbara Lhota and Ira Brodsky. © 2004 by Barbara Lhota and Ira Brodsky. Reprinted by permission of the authors. Originally published in *Forensics Series Volume 3, Duo Practice and Competition: 35 8-10 Minute Original Comedic Plays for Two Females*. All inquiries should be directed to Barbara Lhota and Ira Brodsky at blhota@aol.com; Ibrodsky@hotmail.com

THE DEAD DEPORTEE by Dan O'Brien. © 2003 by Dan O'Brien. Reprinted by permission of the author. All inquiries should be addressed to Beth Blickers, Abrams Artists Agency, 275 Seventh Avenue, 26th Floor, New York, NY 10001. Phone: 646-486-4600 x222. Fax: 646-486-2358. Beth.Blickers@abramsartist.com

DREAMING OF A WHITE HOUSE by Leanna Hieber. © 2004 by Leanna R. Hieber. Reprinted by permission of the author. All inquiries should be addressed to leanna_hieber@yahoo.com

THE FAINTING COUCH by Jill Elaine Hughes. © 2000 by Jill Elaine Hughes. Reprinted by permission of the author. All inquiries should be addressed to jillhughes2@yahoo.com; also see author's Web site at www.jillelainehughes.com

FOUR GLASSES by Marki Shalloe. © 2004 by Martha (Marki) Shalloe. Reprinted by permission of author. All inquiries should be addressed to elmarkilino@earthlink.net or Marki Shalloe, 483 Salem Woods Drive, Marietta, GA 30067.

FUN CITY from *TWINGES FROM THE FRINGE* by Bob Jude Ferrante. © 2004 by Bob Jude Ferrante. Reprinted by permission of the author. All inquiries should be addressed to E-mail: jude@pipeline.com; Web site: http://jude.home.pipeline.com

FUN HOUSE MIRROR by Dori Appel. © 1989 by Dori Appel. Reprinted by permission of the author. All inquiries should be addressed to P.O. Box 1364, Ashland, OR 97520; applcart@mind.net

THE GARY CHAIN by Adam Simon. © 2003 by Adam Simon. Reprinted by permission of the author. All inquiries should be addressed to adamsimon@gmail.com

GENTRIFICATION by Linda Eisenstein. © 1995 by Linda Eisenstein. Reprinted by permission of the author. All inquiries should be addressed to plays@lindaeisenstein.com; Herone Press, 1378 W. 64 St., Cleveland, OH 44102.

GET REAL by Kay Rhoads. © 2004 by Kay Rhoads. Reprinted by permission of the author. All inquiries should be addressed to kayr62@yahoo.com

GO SEE from *OCCUPATIONAL HAZARDS* by Mark McCarthy. © 2005 by Mark McCarthy. Reprinted by permission of the author. All inquiries should be addressed to 1639 W. Fargo Ave., Chicago, IL 60626. E-mail: McCactors@juno.com. Web site: www.McCactors.com

GOD DANCING by Marki Shalloe. © 2004 by Martha (Marki) Shalloe. Reprinted by permission of the author. All inquiries should be addressed to elmarkilino@earthlink.net or Marki Shalloe, 483 Salem Woods Drive, Marietta, GA 30067.

A GOOD SOLID HOME by Barbara Lhota and Janet B. Milstein. © 2003